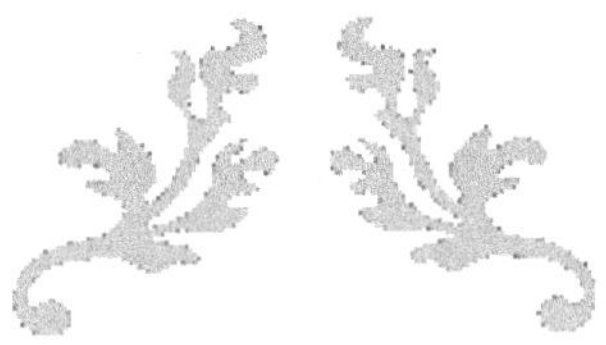

WICCA BOOK OF SPELLS

A Guide to Candle Magic, Herbal Spells, Crystal, Witchcraft and Wiccan Belief

Kevin Patterson

All trademarks inside this book are for clarifying purposes only and are possessed by the owners themselves, not allied with this document.

Disclaimer

All erudition supplied in this book is specified for educational and academic purposes only. The author is not in any way to be responsible for any outcomes that emerge from using this book. Constructive efforts have been made to render information that is both precise and effective. Still, the author is not to be held answerable for the accuracy or use/misuse of this information.

Foreword

I will like to thank you for taking the very first step of trusting me and deciding to purchase/read this life-transforming book. Thanks for investing your time and resources on this product.

I can assure you of precise outcomes if you will diligently follow the specific blueprint I lay bare in the information handbook you are currently checking out. It has transformed lives, and I firmly believe it will equally change your own life too.

All the information I provided in this Do It Yourself piece is easy to absorb and practice.

Table of Contents

INTRODUCTION

This book includes all the details needed for you to grip an understanding of the basics of the Wiccan believe and to discover how to harness the power of nature and to command it to produce the outcomes you desire. As you will know, Witchcraft is a holistic custom that includes all elements of the spiritual and natural world.

Much of the contents are non-denominational and can be practiced by any person of any faith. Consider this book as your initial step towards an understanding of the Craft and make sure you are open-minded to recognize the charm of the Craft and to accept the change it can bring to your life.

CHAPTER ONE

Gainingan Understanding of theCraft

Without a clear understanding and clear definitions of the terms Wicca, you can not easily find your foot to start learning the practices of Witchcraft, magick, and Paganism. Here we begin by explaining the distinctions amongst all these terms to assist you in constructing a foundation of understanding on which to build on as you check out the whole book.

Paganism

Paganism is an umbrella term for several religious beliefs. The term comprisessomespiritual beliefs; it was a term used to describe people who thought in a variety of gods, goddesses, or divine beings. Generally, paganism represents the pre-Christian religions that have come from several ancient traditions.

The Differences between Wicca and witchcraft

The terms 'Wicca' and 'Witchcraft' are often used interchangeably, but there are significant differences between the two.

Wicca

Wicca is a religion, nature-driven, an earth-centered religion. It, therefore, consists of praise of and observance to divine beings and spirits and is related to as a subset of Paganism. Wiccan Rede is the 'one Law' concept of Wicca that can be summed up as 'harm none.'

Witchcraft

Even in the absence belief system centered on spirituality, goddesses, or gods, one can use herbs and spells for protection, love, recovery, and so on, which suggests that even atheists might practice Witchcraft. Because of this, one may be a believer in any religion or none; but still, has the ability to practice Witchcraft as an art of using energy and the power in nature for an end goal. Lots of nations and cultures have their techniques in Witchcraft, and the term much includes there.

Practicing Wicca and Witchcraft.

Witchcraft may be practiced to heal or to destroy. Numerous forms of Witchcraft entail love, recovery, and protection using herbs, minerals, alternative science, and harnessing of energy to perform. Witchcraft is as diverse as lots of cultures of peoples throughout the world and can be high or adverse as the person acting it. The word used to define a person practicing either healing or hurting magick is called 'Witch.'

Thus, there is a difference in intent between Wicca and Witchcraft. Wicca's intent is positioning with the divine and a spiritual journey. At the same time, Witchcraft does not have to consist of spirituality or the divine in any form since spells might be cast, and meditation might be practiced, or herbs used even without calling upon any high spirits or deities. It is easy just to practice Witchcraft without any background in Wicca.

Because of the centuries in history involving the persecution of Witches by Christianity, there is a stigma connected to the title of being a 'witch,' and the word ended up being more of an allegation instead of an accepted title. During such challenging times, those practicing witchcraft wouldn't even recognize themselves as witches or scared of their security, while there is the freedom to determine as a Witch today, the negative undertones that still hover around the word hinder its appropriate use and obscure its real meaning. Many people are very first introduced to the idea of Witchcraft or Wicca through Hollywood movies, and the analysis is a twisted one, not offering the entire accurate picture of the concepts. Witches and Wiccans are both alike in the battles and obstacles they face in their neighborhoods, where they are shunned and even actively battled against for practicing.

Magick

There are several reasons for individuals being drawn towards magic. Some wish to comprehend their place in this vast universe; some are looking for responses to the different questions they have about life and almost everything around it, some others are seeking a life of magic and increased fact, which can be referred to as a life of marvel and mystery.

Let us initially go over why we often discover the term 'magic" and how it is different from the term 'magick.' 'Magick' is a term created by Aleister Crowley, founder of a Pagan religion called Thelema. He used the alternative spelling to distinguish the magic of the occult from that carried out on stages for entertainment. Other spellings have been embraced over time, such as " magick," "Majik," and "magic", but for no specific reason. Hence the term' magick' is mostly unnecessary, and all types are interchangeable, but we have embraced his concept in this book just by preference.

Magick can be loosely explained as the adjustment of the physical world via metaphysics by using ritual action.

Prayers are not viewed as magick; they are demands for magnificent intervention. When the names of Gods or divine beings are used in magick, it can end up being confusing, but it is essential to recognize whether the name is used as a demand or as a word of power.

An Introduction to Charms and spells

Of course, Witchcraft wouldn't be witchcraft without appeals and spells! The emotional drive is a significant source of power when casting spells and charms. It is essential you feel a strong passion for your periods to work, so it becomes a magick to you when it works perfectly.

It is not essential to be a fan of the Wiccan faith to cast spells and appeals. Any person can find out to appropriate way to throw a Circle and work a period of charm efficiently, no matter what their religious beliefs are, if any.

CHAPTER TWO

TheFundamentalsOf TheCraft

The Craft: Beliefs & Worship

All religious beliefs acknowledge a genderless force, a higher power beyond human understanding that we want to interact with to fulfill the request of our inner desires. Each religion has established its own natural life-ruling supreme authority to which they direct their worship.

Considering that Wicca is a religion that is mostly based upon nature, it is only sensible then that the Wiccan deities belong to both feminine and masculine kinds, as all in life manifests itself from this duality. Hence the 'Ultimate Deity' is divided into God and Goddess. Various denominations of Wicca stemming from different traditions have differing names for their divine beings and varying types.

A deity's name is merely a label, what is most important is what the deity represents and the qualities that you are worshipping. You may be sure that the God or Goddess you are praying or worshipping will not be confused as to whom you are resolving!

The Idea of Reincarnation

The belief is quite old and forms a part of diverse religious beliefs, for example, Buddhism and Hinduism. The theory asserts that this soul, spirit, or magnificent fragment is required to undergo all life experiences for the functions of its development. For example, having a look at Mozart, the belief that, at five years old, he likely maintained knowledge from his previous lifetime, allowing him to write concertos of genius type effectively, is a reasonable explanation for the phenomenon that would otherwise make little sense.

Reincarnation may be stretched to numerous examples; let's look at a homosexuality being. Sensations and sexual feelings from a previous life may roll over to the next, describing why some people have tendencies that are thought about 'abnormal' by scientific analyses.

In Wicca practice, it is a belief that not only humans have souls, but all things. Some religions believe there is an idea of rebirth in different ways, a human in this life, an animal, or a plant in the next life.

To describe the truth that the population is growing, Wicca acknowledges that there are also births of new souls, and therefore existing in us are either 'old' souls, which have been reincarnated and experienced several lives or 'brand-new' souls, which are starting their journey of experience.

Three Fold Retribution

An idea intimately linked to reincarnation is the idea of retribution or 'Karmic action.' Karmic action is considered a system that spans throughout the lifetime of a soul, in which any evil done by you in one lifetime will come at the expense through punishment in the next lifetime.

Wiccan beliefs, retribution takes place, not across several lifetimes, but within the same lifetime, which implies that Wiccan belief your benefit or penalty for the way you have lived your life is not gotten after death, instead, throughout your lifetime as you live it. Where things get even more fascinating in Wicca is that the Wiccan belief system is based on not only retribution for actions, however three-fold retribution, A three-fold retaliation means that for every good you do, you will have the opportunity of being rewarded three times as much. On the other hand, for any evil you do, you are punished three times as much. Naturally, it is not actual, but the principle is such.

The Wiccan system of belief then asserts that the experiences of a previous lifetime do not determine a life time's experience, and there may or might not be resemblances between the experiences throughout your present lifetime.

CHAPTER THREE

Channeling Your Focus

Every individual has what is known as 'psychic abilities,' that is, a capability beyond physical ability, of higher consciousness. While mental capacity may be apparent in some, it does not indicate those who don't show these abilities don't possess it; it merely shows that it is inactive.

For example, you would need to evaluate it by exerting your strength in different methods, and by carrying out various tasks according to your psychic ability. To discover your psychic abilities, you have to check it and carry out different tasks.

Channeling is a way of taking advantage of your higher awareness, allowing you to get otherwise unattainable information.

Mental Channelingand Physical Channeling

There are two significant categories channeling ability falls under. These two categories are Mental and Physical.

Physical Channeling-- this relates to an impact on material objects. Activities including radiesthesia (the pendulum), cartomancy (card reading), tasseography (tea-leaf reading) and psychometry, are physical channeling activities.

Psychological Channeling-- this associate with impressions that are gotten in conscious awareness, at some level. This classification covers activities like clairsentience (sensing), clairvoyance (clear seeing), clairaudience (hearing), and telepathy (idea transfer). Also included herein are retrocognitive and precognitive functions in the present time.

Trance Channeling& Conscious Channeling

There are likewise two types of channeling that exist. These types are 'trance' channeling and conscious channeling. Within the category of trance' channeling, there are deep, medium, and light states of trance. If a channeler happens to be in a daze, the conscious mind is not engaged throughout the channeling process, and the channeler will not recall any details or know what they are seeing or saying throughout the time they are transporting.

In conscious channeling, however, as it suggests, the conscious mind actively takes part in the channeling. This indicates that the brain is analyzing the data that the higher conscious receives, it examines and gets involved by facial expression, body language, and voice inflection.

Ending up being a Channel

To harness your channeling capabilities and begin channeling, it is needed first to eliminate all challenges in mind. Your mind is occupied with accumulated problems, things like inhibitions, indecision, uncertainty, criticism, and incorrect values and all sorts of things that have developed and settled over your lifetime. These things hamper the circulation of energy and info in your mind, tying up our psychic capability.

The Focus of the Conscious Mind

Mind Control

To begin putting things in order right in your mind and to communicate with your higher awareness, it is vital to learn the art of focusing and controlling your account. That is an indication that you require to start targeting if you have numerous ideas running through your mind at once. Spread ideas result in spread energy, which implies that when you believe you are focusing on something, you are, in fact, just giving it a small part of your strength. Controlling mental energy enables you to use your undistracted attention on something, offering you power. This power can be compared to a force of production, which you can use to bring your magic to life.

Elimination of Emotions

It is essential to attain the complete elimination of these toxic emotions to get real spiritual quality. Unlimited love offers no space for envy, hate anger, or greed.

Continuous Self-Examination

When seeking truth, it is needed to undergo consistent self-assessment. It is very to determine what your beliefs and ideas are and to attain concise morals for yourself. Develop your objectives, define them plainly, and identify specific items to work towards. Afterward, it is needed that you prioritize your goals and pursue them in the order you have attentively put them in.

Getting rid of Materialism

Things and people tend to rule over your affairs, acting as though they are servants. These things take money and time, tying you down and complicating your life.

Learn Genuine Love

Learning how to love genuinely is essential, and many misconceptions are surrounding this idea. Love itself is sometimes mistaken as self-centered, or lustful. A greater love does exist, one which is unselfish and has to do with the release, instead of the attachment. Love has to do with understanding and forgiving. It is necessary to acknowledge that every individual has their course to follow and lessons to discover to walk their journey at their speed.

Learn the Art of Meditation

The art of meditation is best understood as a process through which you can listen to your higher self. Meditation assists with concentration and with focussing attention on the higher level of awareness that is present in every one of us. A daily period of reflection can clear the mind of clutter and preserve a clear channel of communication.

CHAPTER FOUR

The Basics Of Meditation

Meditation can best be described as 'listening.' When appropriately used, meditation leads to individual improvement. Meditation is the most basic of all the techniques of spiritual growth, and it may be practiced in a group or even alone.

Meditation is a practice that quietens our conscious mind, the mind which is interested in everyday activities and life as you understand it. It enables you to transmit your higher consciousness, also regarded as subconsciousness, the part of your mind that is accountable for uncontrolled physical functions, reflex actions, and what you might call 'Universal Memory.'

The Dynamics of Meditation

To understand the dynamics of meditation, initially, the make-up of the human consciousness needs to be recognized, and it also needs to be acknowledged that people are both spiritual and physical beings. These two elements of humanity are connected at the interpretive centers, which are described by their Sanskrit descriptions-- Chakras. Throughout the act of meditation, psychic energy travels through these chakras. The kundalini force is a potent force referred to as the 'Serpent Power,' and as soon as the kundalini streams within you, your chakras begin opening up in succession.

Mastering Meditation

You can stop working at meditation if you approach the art with the wrong technique, and even by merely contacting the art without any strategy at all.

The direction you focus on also plays an essential role in the strategy of the Third Eye meditation method. Targeting your eyes straight outwards has to do with your conscious mind, while focusing downward relates to the subconscious mind.

When carrying out meditation, it is best to pick a position of your choice to meditate in. Traditionally, meditation is understood to be carried out in the lotus position. However, this position is not always a comfortable one, and so it is much better to be comfortable in another area of your own choice.

When you are choosing an area in which to perform your meditation, it is imperative that the excellent location is peaceful, and the very best option will, of course, be your cleaned and censed circle. If you select another area for whatever reason, it is best if you cleaned the city and get it censed as you did with your Circle. While it is not necessarily essential to face particular instructions in meditation, it is sometimes recommended to deal with the east. What is of many top priority is your comfort, and so if you have a much better view in other instructions, feel free to deal with that way rather!

With regards to the position you choose and the instructions you deal with as well as the area you select, you also are free to select the time of day you practice meditation. It is best to stick to that particular time of day every day to practice meditation so that your reflection is consistent. Thus, it is best to select the most convenient time, one that will be peaceful and peaceful; however, still achievable every day.

To remain active and succeed in meditation, it needs to be done consistently. Some suggest that meditation is performed between fifteen and twenty minutes a day, twice a day. At the bare minimum, you might

most likely manage with a single fifteen-minute session each day. Again, consistency is essential-- so it is essential to stay with the variety of courses and to the times also.

Performing Meditation

Step-By-Step Meditation Method

1. Position yourself well without bending your back.

2. Let your head roll forward onto your chest. Repeat three times.

3. Let your head roll backward. Take a deep breath in and out. Repeat three times. Go back to the initial standing position.

4. Let your head fall to the left as far as possible. Repeat three times.

5. Let your head fall to the right as far as possible. Take a deep breath in and out. Repeat three times. Return to the initial upright position.

6. Allow your head to fall forward again; today, move it counterclockwise in a circle. Repeat three times.

7. Let your head fall forward more, then move it clockwise in a circle. Repeat three times.

8. Breathe in some short intakes of breath, up until your lungs are filled, ensuring that you are breathing through your nose. Repeat three times.

9. Breathe wholly and slowly, in through the right nostril while holding the left closed. Enable your stomach to push out. Hold the breath briefly, and after that, exhale carefully and gradually from the mouth, flattening your stomach. This is a good exercise for removing stagnant air from the bottom of your lungs. Repeat three times.

10.   Breathe slowly and totally, in through the left nostril while holding the left closed. Enable your stomach to balloon out. Hold the breath briefly, and then exhale carefully and gradually from the mouth, flattening your stomach. Repeat thrice.

Now that your body is well relaxed and you are breathing profoundly but usually focus the ideas in your mind and envision your whole body surrounded by a world of white light. Feel the energy in your entire body.

Now ensure you focus your attention on your toes. Relax them and feel the tension or the tiredness escape from them.

Relax your whole body entirely, focussing on releasing the tension from it a section at a time. Do not forget your eyes and even your scalp. The relaxation process is to end at your forehead.

Now, focus your energy on your 3rd eye. Permit your eyes to roll up if possible. Enable your energy to flow from inwards to outwards and to a higher power.

In the beginning, your conscious mind is unrestrained, and it may be difficult for you to quiet it, like a nagging child. However, with practice and consistency, you will ultimately begin to see outcomes in the form of a deepening in instinct, and this will be evidence of your Kundalini awakening.

It is not uncommon for novices to have trouble staying still in the beginning for more than a few minutes at any given time. It is usual for your mind to desire to roam and for you to feel like fidgeting. Very typical is the establishing of a massive itch that genuinely needs to be scratched! Overlook all these things as much as you can, and soon you will be in control of your mind and your body. It is a stringent process, but it is a transition from allowing your body and mind to rule over you, and now you attempt to rule over your body and mind.

Ending a Meditation Period

It is for the best interest of your physical well-being that you end each session of meditation by re-awakening your physical and conscious self. This is just done by carrying out the relaxation technique in reverse, which indicates pulling away from the pineal eye and continuing down the length of the body, section by section, making them each vibrant and awakened.

You may be amazed by how pleasant you will feel after you perform meditation using the proper strategy. Therefore there are not only spiritual benefits but physical also.

The Coven

There are mostly individual witches, and some witches choose to work in groups, which are designated as 'covens.' A coven is typically no more than thirteen, which is the conventional size of a coven, but it may be much smaller or larger than this.

Forming a Coven

The leaders of a coven are regarded as the priests of the coven. Such leaders have no more power than the others in the coven, but merely are leaders as all members of the coven get involved. According to your choice, those in your coven may be called their Witch name and 'Lad' or 'Lord' or only by their Witch name alone. Once again, it is a matter of choice.

There used to be one book per coven, but today it is not unusual for each Witch to own a personal Book of Shadows. Make one book for yourself from binding in any color of your choice and add pages of any style you choose, even crafting your paper from scratch if you would like. Fill the book with routines you want to carry out in your Circle and guarantee that it is written so plainly that you can read it in the candle.

Rituals As a Blueprint

The Initial Purification Ritual

This is to be carried out on the night of the New Moon.

1. Fill a flat bowl with water.

2. Kneel down and then place the water in front of you.

3. Place the forefinger of your right hand or left hand, if you happen to be left-handed into the water.

4. Visualize a brilliant beam of light streaming from the top and into the crown of your head. Imagine the shaft surging through your whole body and direct it through the arm you are using to reach the water. Picture the light spilling into the water through your finger.

5. Channel all the power you can into the water, with your eyes closed if it helps to focus.

Now shout out the following lines:

"Here do I purposefully direct my power, through the representatives of the God and the Goddess, into this water, that it might be clean and pure, as is my love for the Lord and Lady."

6. Take a teaspoon of sea salt; put it into the water and stir clockwise nine times with your finger. Chant the following three times:

"Salt is Life. Here is Life. Sacred and new; without strife."

7. Now put your fingers into the water and spray every corner of the temple room with the purified water. If there are cabinets or alcoves, sprinkle water in each of those corners, and chants the following mantras.

"Ever as I go through the ways, Do I feel the presence of the Gods. I understand that in aught, I do. They are with me

They abide in me.

And I in them, Forever

No evil shall be amused

For pureness is the resident

Within me and about me.

For great do I make every effort

And for great do I live—love unto all things.

Be it, Forever."

8. Next, it's time to light some incense. Take time to swing the burner in every corner, as was done with the sprinkling of the water. Repeat the following mantra three times:

"Salt is Life. Here is Life. Sacred and new; without strife."

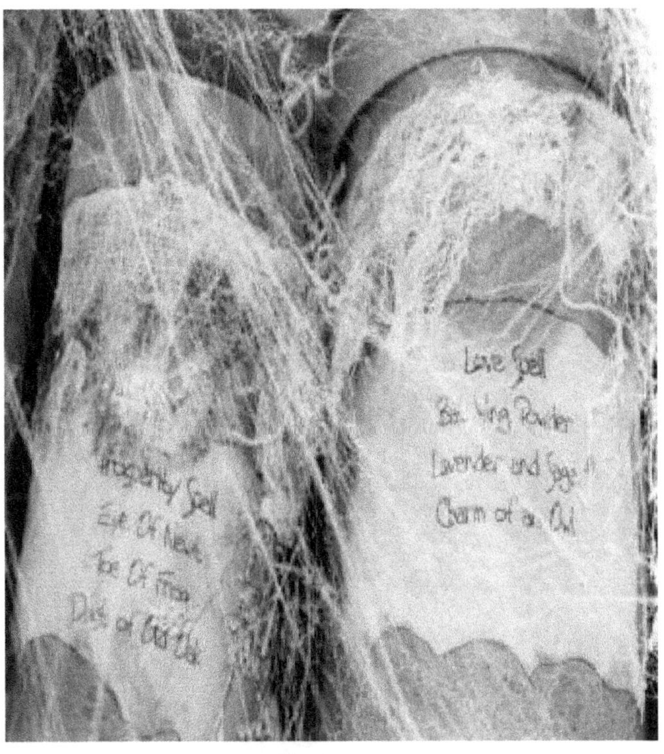

The Sacred Circle.

Circles have been used in several religions and cultures faiths as a limit marking of sacred space, or as a classification of area for rites; rings keep the unwanted out and hold the wanted in the Circle. In Witchcraft, the Circle is a spiritual space within which the magickal power and energy are retained and concentrated.

There are instances in witchcraft when an exact Circle is required; however, that is just during Ceremonial Magick. Usually, accuracy is not required, but it is continuously good practice to show care abundantly and to do our best in making it as precise as possible. The measurements of the Circle being drawn depend on how many coven members will be within the circle and, likewise, the function of the ring. When magick is to be carried out within the circle, the sword needs to follow correctly on the right marking of the circle, and the enhancing of the energy in the Circle may even be carried out twice (but censing and spraying for the 2nd reinforcement is not needed).

The Circle Size.

What is most crucial when considering the actual size of the circle has to do with whether the ring comfortably fits the number of members that will be within it. Members ought to outstretch and move outwards up until their arms are extended to the optimum, and this has to be the ideal size of the Circle to be marked.

Drawing the Circle.

The illustration of the Circle must start at the east each time, and of course, end in the east. Outdoors; the circle can be marked with the point of a sword straight on the ground; While, when indoors, first mark the ring either with a cord, chalk, or even have a long-term marked circle on the ground if it is an irreversible temple ground. The marked circle is then charged with magickal energy or power by the Priest or Priestess walking the marking, directing his/her energy into the ring, using the sword's point.

On the Circle marking itself, erect four candles. The candles are explicitly positioned in the north, east, south, and west. For extra illumination or a preferred environment, other candles may be lit and placed in between these points, beyond the Circle.

Entry & Re-Entry of the circle during the working of Magick, it is vital that the Circle is not broken. In other instances, it is not chosen that any member leaves the Circle, but if it needs to be done, it is possible. There is a specific way by which the Circle is entered and left.

Leaving the Circle.

Position yourself in the East, with the athame held in hand. Make a move with the athame as though you plan to cut across the lines of the circle, starting on your right and then going to yours. You now might leave the Circle in between those lines. If preferred, you might picture a gateway that you have developed, in the east, through which you pass.

Re-entry of the Circle.

Need to you wish to return to the Circle, you go into through the very same gateway or doorway you think of that you have cut in the eastern side of the Circle. It is required to 'close' the opening behind you-- this is done by reconnecting the' cut' lines. When trying to reconnect the edges of the Circle, it is imperative to take note that three lines were in truth cut-- one that is made with the point of the sword, another made with the salted water and another made with the censing. Proceed to reconnect the lines by moving the athame blade across the borders up and down.

Kiss the tip of your athame and go back to your initial position in the Circle.

Clearing/ Setting up the Temple

This has to do with the opening and closing of the Circle, but can be referred to as the clearing and setting up of the Temple.

Erecting the Temple or Opening the Circle: This ritual is carried out at the beginning of every conference. Before building the temple, you will have your circle marked on the ground with candles at each quarter.

Step One: If your temple is not a permanent one, place a couple of altar candles, as per your choice, the incense burner, salt and water dishes, representations of the divine beings, anointing oil, goblets of white wine or juice, your tools, and the libation dish.

Step Two: In addition to the altar candles, the center lights the incense in the burner or thurible. At this moment, the four candles on the Circle are not yet lit. He then leaves the area to join the rest at the coven in north-eastern of the Circle.

Step Three: The designated priest and priestess go into the circle firstly and stand right before the altar. The priest then rings a bell, giving it three rings. The priest or priestess states the following:

"Be it understood that the Temple would be erected; the Circle is about to be cast. Let those who want attendance collect in the east and wait for the summons. Let no one be present here but of their own free choice."

Step Four: The priestess and the priest take the candle each, and they walk around the altar. Moving to the east. The priestess then lights the East candle on the circle from the lit altar candle she carries with her. As she lights the candle she states;

"Here, I bring air and light in at the east, to illuminate our temple and bring a breath of life."

Step Five: The priestess and priest light the south candle of the Circle, saying:

"Here, I bring fire and light in at the south, to illuminate our temple and make warmth available to it."

Step Six: The priestess and priest move west, where the priestess now lights the west candle, saying:

*__"Here, I bring water and light in at the west, to
illuminate our temple and wash it."__*

Step Seven: The clergyman and priestess move north, where
the north candle is lit by the priest, who states: *__"Right here do
I bring light and earth is at the north, to brighten our
temple as well as to develop it in strength."__*

Step Eight: The priest and priestess moves to the east and back
to the altar, finishing the Circle, and also changing the altar
candles.

Step Nine: Either the priest or priestess lift the athame or
sword and go back to the east. With the sword point on the
eastern of the Circle, the priest or priestess progressively walks
the solid line, focusing power and also power through his/her
sword point into the Circle line.

Step Ten: Once done, he or she returns to the church. She or he
ring the bell three times.

Step Eleven: The priest places the tip of his athame right into
the salt and states: As salt is life, let it detoxify us in all ways we
may use it. Allow it to clean our bodies and also spirits as we
commit ourselves in these rites, to the splendor of the Goddess
and the God.

Step Twelve: The priestess takes out the salt dish and also uses
the tip of her athame to go down three stacks of salt right into

the water. The priestess mixes the salted water with the same athame and also states:

Let the Sacred Salt drive out any type of contaminations in this water, that we may use it throughout these ceremonies.

Step Thirteen: The priest takes the scent heater while the priestess gets hold of the salted water. Each walk around the altar starting at the east, slowly strolling clockwise around the circle, with the Priest passing the incense along the significant ring, as well as the priestess scattering saltwater along the line. When they return to their beginning point at the east, they return to the altar and change the tools.

Step Fourteen: The priest and a pinch of the salt into the anointing oil, stirring it in with his finger. The priest blesses the priestess with the Keltic Cross in Circle if she is robed, or the Pentagram and Inverted Triangle if skyclad. He states:

In the name God and also the Goddess, I consecrate thee, bidding you welcome to this their Temple. They admire.

Step Fifteen: The priestess goes ahead to anoint the Priest with the oil and pronounces the very same words, adhered to by a salute. The priest and the priestess then move with each other to the eastern, with the priestess lugging the oil and the priest bringing his athame.

Step Sixteen: The priest makes two cuts throughout the line of the Circle with his athame, signifying the 'opening' of the Circle. The priestess anoints males, and the clergyman blesses women.

Be consecrated in the names of God and also the Goddess, bidding you welcome to this their Temple. Merry meet.

Step Seventeen: After the last participant goes enters, the priest shuts the Circle using his athame to cross throughout the line, connecting the 'damaged ends' of the Circle. The priest increases his athame and attracts a pentagram, sealing it. The priest and also priestess go back to the altar.

Step Eighteen: The priestess or priest states the following:

May you all be right here in tranquility as well as in love. We bid you welcome. Let now the Quarters be saluted and also the gods welcomed.

Step Nineteen: The member of the coven who is closest to the east turns outward faces the east candle of the Circle, elevating his/her athame. She or he draws an invoking pentagram, specifying:

All hail to the aspect of Air; Watchtower of the East. Might it stand in strength, ever before overseeing our Circle?

She or he kisses the blade of his/her athame and go back to the Circle.

Step Twenty: The participant of the coven closest to the south turns outside as well as bargains with the south candle of the Circle, elevating his/her athame. She or he draws a conjuring up pentagram, specifying:

All hail to the facet of Fire; Watchtower of the South. May it stand in stamina, ever seeing over our Circle.

She or he kisses the blade of his/her athame and also moves back to the Circle.

Step Twenty One: A member of the coven who is closest to the west turns outside and faces the Circle's west candle raising his/her athame. She or he attracts a conjuring up pentagram, stating:

All hailstorm to the element of Water; Watchtower of the West. May it stand in toughness, ever before managing the Circle.

He or she goes ahead to kiss the blade of his or her athame and goes back to the Circle in readiness for the next step.

Step Twenty-Two: A member of the coven closest to the north turns outside and also encounters the Circle's north candle, raising his/her athame. She or he draws an invoking pentagram, saying:

All hail storm to the facet of Earth; Watchtower of the North. May it stand in strength, ever before monitoring our Circle.

She or he kisses the blade of his/her athame and go back to the Circle.

Step Twenty-Three: The priestess or The priest elevates his/her athame and attracts a pentagram, specifying the following:

All hail the four Quarters and also all hail the Gods!

All coven participants sign up by saying, ***"All hailstorm!"***

Step Twenty-Four: The priest or priestess states:

Let us share the Cup of Friendship.

The priest takes the goblet of red wine or juice and places a little directly onto the ground or into the libation dish, in the name of the gods. He takes the first sip and passes it to the priestess. The priestess takes a sip and also gives the cup to the coven member on her left. Therefore it continues till it is gone back to the altar. Bear in mind that it is the initial person who puts the drink just. The bell seems three times.

Step Twenty-Five: The priestess states: Now we are all here and is the Temple established up. Allow none leave, however, with superb reason, till the Temple is cleared. Mote It Be.

All participants repeat, "So Mote It Be!"

Clearing of the Temple or Closing of the Circle or This is carried out at the end of every conference;

Step One: The priest or priestess states: We came together crazy as well as relationship; allow us part the very same technique. Allow us to spread the love we have understood this Circle exterior to all, sharing it with those we meet.

The priest or priestess after that increases his athame or sword in salute. All participants then raise their athames.

Step Two: The clergyman or priestess states: Lord and also Lady, our thanks to you for sharing this moment. Our thanks for monitoring us, safeguarding, and

helping us in all points. Love is the Law, as well as Love, is the Bond. Merry did we meet; merry do we component; merry might we rejoin.

All members state: "Merry meet; jolly part; jolly reunite."

Step Three: The clergyman or priestess state: The Temple is currently gotten rid of.

Mote it be.

All members state: "So Mote It Be!"

Step Four: All members of the coven kiss their athame blades—participants after that walk the Temple to kiss each other farewell.

The Consecration Ritual

Your tools, as well as your priceless fashion jewelry, bring various vibrations in them, therefore prior to they can be used, it is needed that you execute an anointing ritual to commit them to your function of Witchcraft and also Magick and to clean them. The treatment is to spray and also to cense the items. Sea salt is initially charged with power and then blended with water to make what we can call 'Holy Water' for lack of a far better term. This water incorporated with the scent smoke act as spiritual, cleansing reps.

As soon as, Consecration of a product is done simply. The first action is to cast a Circle. Adhere to the routine and also presume as the action where you state: "Now is the holy place set up. I will certainly not leave it, however, with great factor. Be it."

Let's start from here, you proceed with the anointing routine as complies with: The

Consecration Ritual Step-by-Step

Hold the product you are consecrating up high in salute and also state: God and also

Goddess;

Lord as well as Lady;

Papa and Mother of All Life.

Below do I supply my device for your authorization.

From the materials of nature, it has been made; Wrought right into the kind you see now.

Place the product on your altar and kneel or mean a long time with your head bowed in respect as well as consideration over the building and construction of the product and also reviewing the little points you did to personalize the product.

Dip your fingers in the salty water and spray the product. Turn it over and also repeat

Get the item and also hold it in the scented smoke, engulfing it. State the following:

May the Sacred Water and also the smoke of the Holy Incense remove any kind of contaminants in this blade That it be cleansed and pure,

Prepared to offer me as well as my gods in any technique I choose. So mote it be.

Holding the item in your hands direct all the energy you can muster towards the product.

With the knowledge as well as might of the God and also Goddess.

Might it serve us well, maintaining me from injury, as well as acting in their solution, in all things?

Mote it be.

Shut the Circle by elevating the now consecrated thing in your right-hand man, as well as state the following: My thanks to the gods for their involvement.

May they ever before monitor me, safeguarding and also assisting me in all that I do Love is the Law, as well as Love, is the Bond.

Be It.

The routine is now total. You require to keep the product on your individual for twenty-four hours after the method and also copulate the item underneath your cushion for three nights straight. Nobody is to obtain your product for usage, whether within or out of the Circle, though it could be held, touched as well as looked at by them.

CHAPTER SIX

The Principles Of The Craft As It Relates To Birth, Death & Marriage

Marriage in Wicca

In Wiccan belief, instead of a marital relationship like that of Christendom, where a couple is bound for the period of their lives up until "death do us part," the Wiccan wedding is one that dedicates a man and woman to each other only for as long as they like each other. If it occurs that they, later on, find they have fallen out of love with each other, the man and woman easily separate without any threat of 'sin' or the like. This is a convenient arrangement as relationships often progress, and nobody desires to be forced into remaining with a partner they no longer want to be with.

The Wiccan marriage ceremony is called the Handfasting Ceremony.

In modern times, the majority of individuals prefer to draw up their own Handfasting rites.

Here we will supply the Seax-WiccaHandfasting rite as a standard-- feel free to either follow the rituals as they are or to use them as a standard for developing your own Handfasting rite.

Seax-WiccaHandfasting Rite

The ideal time for performing the Wiccan marriage ceremony is actually during the waxing of the Moon. It is good to have flowers decorating the Altar and the inside of the Circle, if possible. It is likewise more suitable for all coven members to be skyclad for the Handfasting rite.

If the particular coven is usually robed and does not wish to be skyclad, it is recommended that at least the Bride and the Groom be skyclad throughout the rite.

Much like the 'conventional' marriage being held in modern times, so too are rings exchanged in the Seax-Wiccan standard wedding. The rings are typically bands crafted from gold or silver and inscribed with the Bride and Groom's witch names on the rings in runes. At the start of the rite, these rings are to rest at the Altar, with The Priapic Wand.

The Handfasting Rite Step-By-Step-Perform the Opening of the Circle orSetting up of the Temple.

The priest and priestess kiss; A coven member then says: There are those in our midst who seek the bond of Handfasting.

The Priestess then says, "Let them be named and brought forward."

The coven member responds with," [Groom's witch name] is the Man and[Bridetobe's witch name] is the Woman."

The woman and man in question move across the Altarto stand to face the priest and priestess, with the Groom opposite the priestess and the Bride opposite the priest

The Priestess asks the Groom, "Why are you here?"

The groom responds., "IwishaHandpartingfrom[Wife's name]"

The Priestess asks, "What is your desire?".

The groom shares, "To be made one with [Bride-to-be's name], in the eyes of the Gods and the Wicca."

Now the Priest relies on the Bride. He asks, "Are you [name]."

The Bride reacts, "I am.".

The Priest asks, "What is your desire?".

The Bride answers, "To be made one with [Groom's name], in the eyes of the gods and the Wicca.".

The Priestess grabs the sword and raises it high. The Priest hands over the Priapic Wand to the Bride and Groom, who hold it with both sides between them.

The Priestess states, "Lord and Lady, here before you stand two of your folk. See, now, that which they have to declare."

The Priestess places the sword back onto the Altar, takes her athame, and then holds the tip of it to the chest of the Groom.

She says to the Groom: "Repeat after me:

'I [Groom's name], do come here of my own free choice, to look for the partnership of [Bride's name] I add all love, honor, genuineness, wanting just to turn into one with her whom I like. Continually will I strive for [Bride-to-be's name]'s joy and well-being. I will defend her life before mine. May the athame be plunged into my heart if I am not sincere in all.

I swear this all in the names of the gods. May they offer me the strength to keep my oath.

The Priest lowers his athame, and the Priestess takes the rings from the Altar and sprays them both with salted water and census them with the thurible. She then passes the Bride's ring to the Groom and the Groom's ring to the Bride. The man and woman take them in their right-hand, holding the Priapic Wand with their left.

The Priest states: As the grass of the fields and the trees of the woods flex together under the pressures of the storm, so too must you both bend when the wind blows strong. As you provide love, so will you get strength.

The Priestess then says: Know you that no two people can be exactly alike. There will be some periods when it will seem harsh to give and to love diligently. See then your reflection as in a forest pool: when the image you see looks irate and unfortunate, then is the time for you to smile and to love (for it is not fire that puts out the light).

The Priest then states: Ever love, help and respect each other, And then know sincerely that you are one in the eyes of the gods and of the Wicca.

All coven members state, "So Mote It Be!".

The Priest then takes the Priapic Wand from the Bride and Groom and returns it to the Altar. The Groom and Bride then kiss the Priest and the Priestess across the Altar and move around the Circle to accept congratulations from the coven members.

Handparting Rite

Many faiths see marriage as a one-time lifetime commitment, indicating the couple are to stay together no matter the conditions or circumstances and even if they don't love each o the many more.

In the Wiccan belief, casual partnerships are not encouraged, but it is accepted that with time, relationships change, and husband and wife may no longer be happy being together later. After all attempts at salvaging the relationship are first made, then the last hope is a Handparting event, which can be likened to a divorce.

Before carrying out the rite, the partner and wife sit with the Priest and Priestess to come up with reasonable departments of their possessions and to organize assistance for kids if there are any. Ascribe is available to record everything. If either of the lovers can not be available for whatever reason, their position might be represented by another Witch of the same sex if there is a signed agreement from the missing party, and the wedding event ring.

The Handparting Rite Ste-By-Step

- The Opening of the Circle or Erecting of the Temple is performed.
- The Priestess and Priest Kiss.
- A coven member then says, " [Other half's name] and [Spouse's name], stand forth.".

- The spouses move forward to stand before the Altar, with the Husband in front of Priestess, and the Wife in front of Priest.

- Priestess asks the Husband, "Why are you here?".

  The Husband answers, "I want a Handparting from [Partner's name] The Priest now asks the Wife, "Why are you here?".

  The Wife responds with, "I wish a Handparting from [Other half's name].

- The Priestess asks them both, "Do you both desire this of your own free choice?".

The couple responds with, "We do.".

- The Priest asks, "Has a settlement been reached between you relating to the sharing of property and care of the children?".

The Husband and Wife react, saying, "It has.".

- The Priest asks, "Has this been appropriately recorded, signed, and also witnessed?".

Now the covener Scribe verifies, saying, "It has.".

- The Priest then says, "Then let us proceed, keeping in mind that we stand ever before the gods.".

- The Husband and the Wife join hands and then repeat the following together, line by line, after the Priestess:

"I, [Name], do at this moment most freely dissolve my union with [Spouse's name], and I do so in all honesty and genuineness, before the gods, with my brothers and sisters of the Craft as witnesses. To one another, let all ties be loose, but ever will we maintain respect for one another, as we have love and regard for our fellow Wiccans.

- The Priest then makes the announcement, "Hand part!".

- The couple releases their hands earlier joined together, remove their rings, and give to the Priestess. The Priestess sprays the rings and census them. The Priestess then specifies, "In the names of the Gods do I clean these rings.".

- The priestess then returns the cleansed rings to the man and lady to do with them as they please.

- The Priestess states, "Now are you handpainted. Let all understand you as such. Split in your diverse ways in Peace and Love-- never in bitterness-- and in the ways of the Craft. Mote, it be."

All coven members repeat, "So mote it be.".

- After the routine, follows Ale ritual and Cakes, then cleaning of the Temple or closing of the Circle.

Birth Rite-- Wicanning.

Witches don't believe in coercing or forcing the Craft on anybody, not even their children. Children are taught the methods of the Craft and may also be initiated when they are old enough to make their choice, and they might then either continue practicing the Craft or give it up. No second initiation is required if they resume the Craft later.

A ritual is generally carried out for a kid for the parents to ask the gods to monitor them, protect them, and assist them. The routine may be performed at any time, at any other ritual, and even on its own. Similar to any ritual, first is the erecting of the Temple, then the routine, then the Cakes and Ale and the Clearing of the Temple.

The Birth Rite Step by Step

- The Priestess and Priest kiss.

- A coven member states: "There is an addition to our number. Let us give her/him due welcome.".

- The parents of the beginner position themselves across the Priest and Priestess, on the other side of the Altar, holding the child to be started.

- The Priest asks, "What is the name of the child?".

- The mother and father of the child then supply a name by which the child shall be known within the Circle till that time, the child might choose to adopt a new name when older.

- The Priest then says, "We welcome you [Name]."

- The Priestess states, "Welcome, and much love to you.".

- The Priest and the Priestess then proceed to lead the kid's parents clockwise around the circle three times. The Parents then hold the kid above the Altar, as though 'using' the child.

- The parents then state, "We here offer the fruit of our love to the gods. May they guide her/him as s/he grows.".

- The Priestess then dips the tips of her fingers in the salted water, then wipes them carefully across the kid's face. The mother then passes the baby through the incense smoke to cense the baby.

- The Priestess then mentions, "May the Lord and the Lady ever smile upon you.".

- The Priest states, "May they protect you and assist you through this life.".

- The Priestess states, "May they help you select that which is ideal and shun that which is wrong.".

- The Priest states, "May they see that no damage befalls you, or others through you.".

- The Priestess then states to the parents of the child, "We charge you both, in the names of the God and of the Goddess, to lead this kid, by teaching the way of crafting with love and how to honor them by harming none..".

- The Priest then specifies: "Teach him/her of the Lord and the Lady; of this life, of all that preceded and what might follow after. Tell the stories of the gods and teach the history of our Craft. Teach her/him to aim for that perfection which all desire and, when the time is right, hope-- but do not press-- that s/he accompanies us and becomes genuinely among our precious household."

- The mother and father then specify, "All this we will do. So do we pledge.".

- The Priest and Priestess then state together: "We bid welcome to [Name]."

- All coven members then mention, "Welcome!".

* Now follows the path of Cakes and Ale ceremony.

Death Rite-- Crossing the Bridge.

This might be done as a rite in and of itself, in which case it is preceded by the Erecting of the Temple and followed by Cakes and Ale then Clearing of the Temple. If carried out during other routines, it needs to be carried out before Cakes and Ale rite.

- The Priestess and Priest kiss

- Using the horn, a long note is sounded when, by a coven member.

- A coven member states, "The horn is sounded for [Name of departed Witch].

All coven members respond with, "So be it.".

- The priestess then states, "That today [Name] is not with us, here in the Circle, saddens us all. Let us try not too heartbroken. For is this not to show that s/he has fulfilled this life's work? Now is s/he free to move on. We will reunite, never to be afraid. And that will be a time for another event.".

- The Priest then includes, "Let us send out forth our good dreams to bear him/her across the Bridge. May s/he return any moment s/he may want, to be with us here.".

- All members of the coven grab their athames, pointing them at a position behind the Altar, while facing the Priest and the Priestess.

- All members imagine, in their mind's eye, the image of the deceased Witch, as though she is basing on the spot. The members concentrate on carrying pleasure, joy, and love from their innermost being, through the line of their athame and out of the point into the envisioned body.

- This continues for a couple of moments. Completion is indicated by the Priestess when she changes her athame and states: "We sincerely wish you all the Love and Happiness. We will never forget you. Do not forget us. Whenever we meet here, your presence is always welcome.".

- All coven members then finish by saying, "So mote it be.".

- Now all coven members sit. If there be any member who desires to say a couple of words concerning the departed, they might do so. If there is nobody happy to do so, the

Priest or Priestess must speak kind reminiscent words of the departed Witch, explicitly focusing on happy moments.

- Cakes and Ale event follow the rite.

- 

-

CHAPTER SEVEN

Love and Sex Magick

Concepts of magick involve timing and feeling.

Timing &Magick: As you may not currently understand, the phase of the Moon is essential in working magic properly. The two main aspects of the moon are the "Waxing Moon and the Waning Moon."

Feeling &Magick: As was pointed out in the intro to spells and charm, a deep-set psychological desire for something to happen is essential for magick to be efficient. Putting every minute of your presence into wanting the magick to work is the fuel that drives your magick. Rhyme and chant are tools for magnifying the power of your desire. The balanced chanting serves to increase your sensations and assists you focus on your appetite better. Dance is another amplifier, which can help raise the power behind your magick. Sex is long considered a natural powerhouse for magick, and more will be discussed on sex magick later in this chapter.

Preparing Your Body for Magick

Having a clean body is very crucial before working magick. A tidy collection is accomplished through both external and internal cleaning. Bathing the body is, of course, the initial step, and it is suggested to include a teaspoon of sea salt to the bathing water for cleansing possessions. The inner body is prepared by abstaining from alcohol, sex, and nicotine. This is to be done as a twenty-four-hour quick before you mean to work magick.

The Moon &Magick

Constructive and Destructive Magick

The two words of the moon identify what kind of magick is to be appropriately carried out. Throughout the waxing moon, constructive magick is carried out. Constructive magick includes rituals and spells based on love, security, health, fertility, and success. Naturally, then, during the waning moon, harmful magick is performed, like magick based upon elimination, separation, and extermination, or the casting of binding spells.

Love Magick

This magick is intended for long-term soul mate looking for future partners and is not intended for finding somebody to have a casual affair with. Possibly one of the categories of magick that produces the most interest is love magic when it comes to magick. There is much interest in love potions and love philters, though most of the attention is rooted in fiction. Some love magick spells do work, like the magick, including 'poppets.' Poppets are used to represent the enthusiasts that are in concern, and the idea is that whatever is done to the poppets is done unto the enthusiasts.

The poppet is a specially ready doll made from cloth, even if it is a rough cut figure. While eliminating the fabric and preparing the poppet, it is crucial to be conscious of the individual the doll that is being developed is planned to represent. The baby might be made as elaborately as preferred, such as; embroidery, beadwork and facial functions, etc. are all acceptable. Make the poppet from two pieces of cloth and leave the leading open so it may be packed with herbs. The poppets are to be packed with vervain, verbena, feverfew, yarrow, Artemesia, valerian, rosebuds, motherwort, damiana, or elder, as they are all herbs governed by Venus. Once stuffed, the top may be stitched to seal.

Prepare two poppets in this manner, one male and one female. The preparation is all carried out within the spiritual Circe, and it may be carried out by a singular witch or all coven members.

Since it is an ideal mate that is being looked for, the second figure is to be made with all the qualities desired in them. The poppet is nameless; however, it can display all physical desires and attributes. Once prepared, the poppets lay on the altar, with one at the left-hand side of the sword and the other on the right-hand side. The poppets are to be placed in front of the sword. On the altar, there is to lay a red ribbon, 21 inches long. The petitioner then states,

"O magnificent God and Goddess, Hear now my plea to you.

My plea for real love for [name] and for his/her desire."

The Petitioner then gets the proper poppet and sprinkles the poppet with salted water and cleanses it thoroughly. While doing this, the petitioner states,

"I call this Poppet [petitioner's name] It is him/her in all ways. As she exits, so exists this poppet. Aught that I fix to it, I fix to her."

The petitioner then changes the poppet, to pick up the other one. Just like the previous, it is sprinkled and censed, and the petitioner states,

"This poppet is her preferred mate in every way. As he exits, so exists this poppet. Aught that I fix to it, I fix to him too.".

The petitioner changes the poppet and moves to kneel before the altar with one hand on each poppet. At the point that the poppets fulfill, the petitioner might open his/her eyes and, while holding the poppets deal with to face still, state:

"Thus may they be drawn.

One to the other, Strongly and genuinely.

The poppets need to be laid together on the altar, in the center, with the sword across them, on top of them. The petitioner or the whole coven might now dance around them and work magick for ten minutes, directing the energy of their tune and dance to bring the two represented individuals together. Alternatively, all may sit and meditate on the idea of the two represented coming together.

This routine is best performed on three consecutive Fridays throughout the waxing moon, or maybe even on a Friday, Wednesday then Friday. The complete ritual is meant to be played as almost to the Full Moon as is possible.

On the final Friday, the Petitioner says,

"Now might the Lord and the Lady bind these two together, as I do bind them here.".

The poppets are used up and bound with red ribbon many times around both the poppets, tying the ends together around them. The petitioner then states,

"Now are they forever one, even as the Gods themselves. May each become a part of the other that, separated, they would be incomplete. So Mote It Be!".

As soon as again positioned below the sword and left for some time while the petitioner carries out meditation, the bound poppets are. As soon as the ritual is finished, the poppets are to be covered in a clean white cloth and after that stored thoroughly, never to be unbound.

Sex Magick

Sex magick is an extremely potent form of magick as it is dealing with life forces. Sex magick is about using the power of the orgasm and using that and the entire sexual experience for magickal functions.

i. All aspects of extrasensory understanding to be increased in the course of sexual excitation.

ii. The mind is to be in a state of hypersensitivity before, throughout, and after the climax.

iii. The consistency of peak sexual sensations aids access to the world of the unconscious.

iv. During the height, an experience of timelessness or overall ego dissolution might be experienced, and feelings of being' soaked up' by the sexual partner.

The act of sexual relations is the most natural approach to generate the power required to perform practical magick. The entire process of copulation follows the procedure of beginning slowly and a progressive building up, increasing in rhythm until the final climactic explosion. This act may be carried out within the circle either by a couple or by the whole coven, or even by a solitary witch.

Start as usual, with a period of meditation to focus on what you prefer to accomplish. Take up positions in couples and kneel facing one another. The item is to attain sexual stimulation, and this might be carried out for as long as it is needed and not to be rushed through.

The focus is now to be concentrated on the object of the magick, the function for which it is being carried out. This shift in focus might also assist in delaying climax. This is the time in which both the male and lady fix in their minds an image of the desire and concentrate their energies on it. Feel the power construct.

When the male understands he can not resist the urge to orgasm, he can throw himself back to lie flat on the flooring and launch the power that constructed within him as he climaxes. He must see the power flashing as white light in a line. On climax, she too will fall forwards to lie over her sexual partner.

Obviously, for the singular witch, the act is performed through masturbation, and the longer the orgasm can be held off, the more power is created for completing the magick. For couples, mutual masturbation or foreplay are two alternatives, both producing intense energy.

CHAPTER EIGHT

Quartz Crystal

Crystal, quartz is the second most plentiful mineral in the world, and among the most common stones, you will find in magical supply stores.

Comprised of just two aspects-- silicon and oxygen, it runs in different colors from entirely "clear" to milky white. Clear quartz is discovered as a six-sided prism and is often used in schools to demonstrate the capability of a mineral to hold the whole spectrum of light, kept in the sunshine; the crystal will transfer rainbow patterns onto floors and walls.

The Aztecs, Egyptians, Romans, and lots of other ancient cultures used quartz in a multitude of ways that varied from meditations to funerary rituals, which may have simulated the moonlight shining down on the individuals.

Some understood it as "the Witch's mirror," quartz is connected with both the Moon and the Sun and the Elements of Water and Fire. This stone is a powerful tool for saving energy in the means of thoughts, emotions, and memories, and can be easily "programmed" to activate previously stored energy when hired. Quartz is often used to charge excellent tools and spell components, and can even be used to clean different stones and crystals energetically.

Quartz is also referred to as the "sage" of most minerals as it highly assists with the combining of the spiritual and physical worlds.

Quartz sends and absorbs energy from the Sun as well as from the vital force of plants, flowers, and trees, and like several other crystals, it can be used to rejuvenate struggling plants around the home. Quartz is a fantastic all-around rebalancing stone, changing unfavorable energies with positive ones and keeping harmonious vibrations going strong in any location where it lives.

In this chapter, you'll discover how to use quartz for storing and recovering memories, stimulating divination tools, improving your health, and increasing your energy towards attaining a particular objective.

Crystal Divination Recalibration

Quartz is often used to charge routine and beautiful tools. As a stone of spiritual interaction and psychic ability, it's ideal for improving your divination tools, such as Tarot cards, runes, a pendulum, etc., whenever you can notice their energy has ended up being "fuzzy" or imbalanced in some way. To keep the power-up, the Tarot specialists keep the quartz crystal and cards together. Technically, it is your choice to use any crystal size with any kind of foretelling tools, but it's finest to "match" the two as closely as possible. For instance, a small crystal point may work well when rebalancing a pendulum, but when it concerns a Tarot deck or bag of runes, a more sizable crystal is perfect. You will require:

- One medium to a big quartz crystal
- White candle
- Divination tool(s).

Guidelines:

- Light the candle and invest a couple of moments, silencing your mind.
- When you're ready, put the divination tool in your left hand and the quartz in your right hand.
- Gently bring them together up by colliding them.
- Hold both for at least 1 minute, picture the divination tool being cleared of any unwanted energy, and then renewed using pure quartz energy.
- When you notice the recalibration is done, give thanks to the quartz and place your prophecy tool on the altar.
- Repeat the treatment with any other prophecy tools you wish to rebalance. Gently snuff out the white candle when you have completed it.

Crystal Quartz Memento Charm.

As computer system researchers have been finding, quartz can save info, or "data," in the type of energy. However, it likewise stores emotional info that makes this crystal an exceptional touchstone for pleasant memories that you wish to keep. This spell is an excellent one to explore the energetic properties of quartz. Simply pick a pleasant memory, whether current or from the remote past, and charge the stone with the sensations it highlights in you.

Keep in mind: this works best with pure, clear quartz, so look for as clear stone as possible.

You will need:

- One clear quartz crystal.
- White, pink, or yellow candle.
- Journal or writing paper (optional).

Guidelines:

- Light the candle and invest a long time silencing your mind.
- Start to remember the memory in as much information. You may wish to spend 10 to 15 minutes thinking about it; if it is a memory of a past event, this is guaranteed to raise information you might not be able to gain access to otherwise.

- When you have an excellent grasp on the memory, take the quartz and hold it between your palms.

- With your eyes closed, picture every possible sensory detail about the memory, sights, sounds, tastes, noises, voices, your ideas and sensations at the time, and so on. Concentrate on the feelings that accompanied this memory and feel them again in the present moment.

- Continue to visualize until you feel the warm and positive energy. Then place the flint in front of the candle, leaving it for at least an hour.

- You can now hold the quartz when you want to come into contact with this memory and feel the positive feelings with which you have soaked the stone. You can put it on your altar or any other place where you see it often or carry it with you in your pocket or purse.

Crystal Elixir for Physical Health.

Crystal elixirs, the infusing of water with the vibrations of crystals and other mineral stones, have been used for healing purposes since 3000B.C.E. in numerous cultures. These essential, wonderful potions work through the body's direct absorption of the vibrations of the crystal, creating an alignment between your energy which of the stone picked for the specific purpose.

The quartz power of rebalancing can be used to produce physical regeneration and revitalization in the body by working at the subtle energy level. This elixir is excellent for those who have been feeling short on energy, are recuperating from a minor illness, or would merely like a well-rounded rebalancing "lift" of recovery energy.

Keep in mind: Some stones and crystals are highly hazardous, and need not to be used internally in any method. So if you desire to explore this particular magical method, even more, be sure to do extensive research on any stone you're considering for usage in an elixir!

You will need:

- One little piece of clear quartz.
- A cup of filtered water.

Directions:

- Put the quartz in a little glass of water and leave it in the sunshine for one day. The following day, carry out the ritual healing.
- Carefully remove the quartz from the water and place it on your altar or table.
- Keep the water in the middle of your altar or table.
- Relax and focus by taking three deeper breath

- Take a moment to practice meditation on your body. Let your mind explore your body from top to bottom. Report any place that may require attention.

- Go back to the top place you noticed an imbalance in your body. Concentrate on recovery that is happening and be sipping a glass of water.

- Picture the ancient wisdom and power of the quartz healing that point, releasing any stress, discomfort, or other unwanted feelings.

- Practice this method with any of the body part that needs healing. Permit yourself a minute to feel the vibration of the when you are ended quartz throughout your body, healing and restoring your being.

- You can duplicate this ritual whenever your body requires a boost of recovery energy.

EnergyAmplifierforReachingaGoal

Quartz serves as a power amplifier that aid in achieving a goal. When the heart is set on a specific objective, quartz is a useful magical ally to assist you in crystallizing your will and intent. Whether it's related to affection, career, health, or spiritual development, quartz can accelerate the fulfillment of your desires by enhancing the energy that is set into it.

As you perform this spell, it is necessary to not just think about the end outcome of your goal; however, to direct the energies of sensation pleased and successful with your sign into the stone. You will need:

- One pure, clear quartz crystal.
- Little slip of paper.
- Little drawstring bag.

Instructions:

- Invest some time silencing your mind.
- Concentrate on the goal you have produced yourself.
- Write your objective on the small slip of paper. Remember to be very particular about what you would like to obtain, as this will assist in concentrating the energy on the result you want.
- Use a slip of paper to wrap the quartz
- Ensure you are holding both the quartz and paper in your hand.

- Focus on your goal by envisioning it being completed. How will you feel? What effects or impacts will lead to your life?
- When you have fortified the most detailed and positive visualization possible, place the paper quartz in a sliding

bag and insert it saying the following words (or comparable):

"With the stone of earth and the power of fire. I express the desire of my heart. "

- Put the quartz where it can be close to you in your activities to reach the goal. It could be on your desk, in your purse, in your vehicle, on your computer system, or in a space in your home.

- Repeat this spell with new quartz and a new objective whenever you require it.

Rose Quartz.

Extensively love for its joyful yet relaxing pink shades, increased quartz gets its color from trace quantities of iron, manganese or titanium found within what would otherwise be clear or white quartz. This is another commonly abundant mineral that can be discovered in any magical supply shop, and is frequently made into pendants, rings, pendants, and other fashion jewelry.

Archeological records back to 800 BC reveal that increased quartz was used in jewelry and cosmetics by the Assyrians, Greeks, and Romans. The ancient Egyptians stated that the goddess Isis rubbed rose quartz on her cheeks and around her eyes to protect her appeal. This skin-care technique was a long-held custom in Egypt, and now that crystals have seen a renewal in interest over some years, it has just recently returned into style in the West!

The color pink is believed to be the best symbol for love and empathy, and it can be used for all magical operations associating with these qualities. Many call it the Love Stone, rose quartz opens the heart chakra to allow love to permeate our lives. It aids in healing psychological injury, animosities, regret, and anger.

There is a relationship between water, venus and earth element, as they increased quartz assists to raise self-esteem and self-regard by reminding us to treat ourselves with gentle forgiveness and compassion, and is a very efficient crystal to use during meditation. Increased quartz improves one's inner awareness, teaching us that unconditional love is ever-present, and we just need to be open to receiving the healing energies of the Universe.

Home Energy Transformation Spell

All homes need fairly routine energetic upkeep for the atmosphere to stay perfect. Rose quartz is uniquely fit for this work, as it can replace unfavorable energy with positive energy. This spell will assist you to clean out and repair any pockets of harmful or otherwise undesirable energy in your house. You will be replacing these unfavorable energies with the warm, earthy glow of peace, well-being, and groundedness.

Keep in mind: This spell is powerful on its own, however for even higher effect, attempt sweeping and smearing your house with sage before you start.

You will need:

- One medium to big increased quartz crystal per space or location.
- White candle (optional).

Directions:

- Put the candle at the center of your house and light it if using. Spend a few minutes silencing your mind.
- find a room that is very comfortable fo you
- Place the rose in your hand, focusing on the cold, positive sensation it discharges.
- Now put it on the floor in front of you and visualize pink light radiating outward from the crystal, spreading throughout the space.
- Feel any negative energy being changed by a soothing, caring vibration from the rose quartz.
- When you feel the energy is sufficiently changed, state these words:

" light and lover are constantly present in this area.
All is well.".

- Now pick the quartz up and put it in a safe area room for a continuation of the energy balance.
- Do the ritual again in any room that has unwanted vibrations.

Spell to Release Pain and Unexpressed Emotions.

Often we are not able to express emotions in particular situations or don't have the words to reveal our feelings. Stifling our souls in this method can be an excellent short-term defense reaction, but ultimately it will become a source and fester of unattended negativeness.

Releasing these unpleasant feelings will enable you to process grief or trauma, heal from emotional injuries, and clear your heart space so that you are open to receive love and compassion from deep space and others in your life. This routine can be used for healing from specific past emotional wounds, or for merely clearing more basic psychological clutter from your energy field.

You will need:

- One rose quartz crystal.
- Pink spell candle.
- Lavender necessary oil (optional).

Directions:

- Light the candle and shut your mind in a few minutes
- Use the left hand to hold the quartz. (The left hand enables energy to flow straight to your heart center.) To increase the strength of the spell, you can keep the rose quartz over your heart.
- For 3 minutes, allow your ideas to stream naturally, requesting for anything that needs to be launched to come into your awareness.
- Do not hold on to any specific thought, instead, feel it, accept it, and let it move through you. Offer the crystal your approval to recover and relieve you by radiating love and understanding throughout your body.

- As you breathe, breathe in the soothing essence of the rose quartz, and exhale to allow any stuck energy from past discomfort and trauma to be free.
- Use a lavender oil to anoint the quartz rose by applying one to two drops
- Then bury it in the Earth to clean it from the energies of the old feelings. Leave it there for one whole night.
- You can recycle the stone as frequently as required.

Shining Light Self-Love and Self-confidence Spell

In a society intense on materialism and surface area appearances, the concepts of "self-love" and "self-esteem" can be complicated. Often people want their skills and achievements for sources of self-acceptance, but this technique is missing out on the point entirely.

Real self-love comes from within, when we acknowledge that we are divine beings of light no matter how we appear or what we do (or don't do) in the outside world. Anyone battling with insecurities or self-acceptance needs this spell. Is your choice to practice this spell with a rose quartz or bracelet for an easily-wearable appeal.

You will require:

- One rose quartz crystal (or increased quartz locket/ bracelet).
- One pink candle.
- One orange candle.

Guidelines:.

- Put the rose quartz between the two candles.
- Take a minute to quiet your mind, and after that light, the pink candle, proclaiming these words:

" the light is staring at shines as the love I have for myself shine."

- Now turn on the orange candle, saying the following words:

" This light shines as my self-expression shines.".

- Choose rose quartz and hold it between your palms.
- For a moment, focus on the light shining on the candles and feel the love that comes from the stone in your hands.
- Take a deep breath, close your eyes, and repeat the following words seven times:

" I accept myself. I trust myself. I love myself. From within, I shine for all the".

- Gently snuff out the candles world to see.
- Wear or go around with the rose quartz every day till you feel more rooted in your confident sense of self.
- If you feel the need, you can duplicate the spell occasionally to charge the stone.

Spell To Attract Positive Relationships.

"like attracts like," this is what we learn from the law of attraction and that what we think of identifies what we bring into our experience. This holds in all areas of life but is often most clearly seen when it concerns relationships. Do you feel you are dating the wrong individuals, or discover yourself surrounded by bonds that aren't satisfying, you require to move your energetic vibration to turn this pattern around.

This is much easier said than done; however, if you do not have a great deal of experience with positive, healthy relationships. Whether you're seeking a new buddy or a romantic partner, or both, this spell helps you open yourself as much as assistance from deep space.

You will require:

- Two little increased quartz crystals.
- One pink or white candle.

- Two pieces of writing paper.
- Fire-resistant meal.

Instructions:

- Light the candle and put one increased quartz on either side of it. Take a few minutes to silent the mind.
- On the very first paper, make a note of the qualities of relationships and romantic relationships that have been unhealthy for you in your life. Do not use names or focus on specific people, but rather strive to articulate the actions that have injured you and the resulting feelings from these encounters.
- Do not stay too much on any single incident or individual, and don't enter into more detail than necessary, the point is not to reinforce the unfavorable experiences, but just to recognize and acknowledge what it is that you want to be devoid of in your life.
- When you're through, tear the paper up into a few pieces, and spark them one at a time on the candle flame, taking care not to burn your fingers.
- Drop them into the fire-resistant meal and let them stress out.
- Pick the second paper to compose about what you want to manifest in your future relationship(s). Let the Universe

know what you require in terms of aid in moving these patterns in your life.

- Fold the paper four times and position it in front of the candle when you're finished.
- Place a paper and put the crystals on it and state the following words:

"As I value myself, I bring in others who do the very same.

Let it be.".

- Leave the candle to stretch itself.
- Bury the ashes of burnt paper or scatter them on Earth.
- Keep a folded paper in your magazine, Book of Shadows, or elsewhere, you might call a "list" for the next few weeks and months as new people come into your life.
- If you like, take the crystals with you in your purse or pocket when you go out.

Amethyst.

Another variation of quartz, this magnificent crystal is available in different shades of purple, from pale lavender to lilac and purple. The color is triggered by manganese and iron present in the clear quartz. Many geodesspherical rocks with crystal-lined hollow cavities, add amethyst and clear quartz points clustered together. Amethyst is also sometimes discovered with citrine in the very same crystal. This mix is called ametrine. Amethyst is a relatively abundant mineral. However, the most significant deposits are found in Mexico, Brazil, Uruguay, Russia, France, and parts of Northern and Southern Africa.

In the ancient world, amethyst was mostly understood as a stone that could prevent drunkenness, which we can see in the Greek origins of the name, which equates to "not intoxicate." While it's uncertain precisely why the ancients associated this power to amethyst, they should have sensed its high vibrational frequency, as even today, this crystal is used in alternative recovery to assist with healing from dependency.

Associated with the world Jupiter and the Element of Air, amethyst has a history of helping bring calm and balance to the emotional, physical, and spiritual worlds. It has been known to assist individuals carefully resolve their grief, tame their emotions, and move the previous suffering. It can also push back emotional outbursts and eliminate antagonistic and confrontational attitudes, making it useful in wonderful workings connected to solving disputes of all kinds, even in legal matters. This crystal truly radiates relaxing energy, as anybody who uses amethyst or keeps it around the house can confirm!

The spells listed below make use of the energies of amethyst to assist you in conquering addiction, cultivate persistence and flexibility, smooth over legal trouble, and secure yourself from theft while traveling.

Ritual to Break Free of Addiction.

Amethyst's tranquil, yet highly powerful energies are extensively used in spells, routines, and alternative recovery modalities to treat dependencies of all kinds. This routine concentrates the residential or commercial properties of amethyst into a helpful and protective talisman for you to keep with you as needed to help you stay out of old, unwanted habits.

The "amulet" stated can be a locket, bracelet, ring or anklet with a minimum of one amethyst stone in it, but you can also create your own by wrapping an amethyst securely with yarn, precious jewelry, or twine wire and affixing it to a chain or cord. Many crystal stores also sell pendants with small wire "baskets" into which any stone can be placed.

Remember: if you are not having a good time with a dependency on drugs, alcohol, or disordered consuming habits that presents a risk to your health, please do not count on this spell alone to solve the issue. Instead, believe it as a compelling action along the course to your recovery.

You will need:.

- One amethyst amulet.
- Black or violet candle.
- Two papers.
- Fireproof dish.

Guidelines:

- Light the candle and spend some time silencing your mind. When you feel centered, compose a list of the unfavorable impacts of your routine or dependency on the first paper.

- Hold the stone of the amulet in between your palms, close your eyes, and take three deep breaths, visualizing yourself devoid of the effects you've just noted.

- See how your body and mind enter the bright purple light of the stone, eliminating the old energy patterns that supported your practice.

- Hold the amethyst using the left hand, use your ideal hand to light the paper over the candle flame. Leave it in a bowl to shake, as you say the following words:

*"As I melt my energy with divine power, so do I.
released from this trap; my life is now mine.*

Mote it be."

- Put on your amulet properly and take three more deep breaths.

- Now, on the second piece of paper, compose a list of the positive results that leaving your habit or addiction behind will bring into your life. Allow yourself to feel fired up and eager about these advantages of your newly found flexibility.

- When you're through, fold the paper three times and put it in front of the candle until the candle has burned all the way down.
- Keep the paper somewhere in your home (or carry it in your pocket or handbag) as a reminder of the positive manifestations you are now permitting into your life.
- Put the amethyst amulet in the pocket or wear it whenever you need energy assistance for remaining devoid of your old habit.

Bath Spell for Patience and Flexibility.

Using crystals in cleansing is a terrific way to produce a change in your energy field. If you discover yourself having a hard time with irritability and impatience, as we all do from time to time, this ritual bath can assist soothe those vibrations and restore you to a sense of peace and approval of life's little bumps in the roadway.

Adding necessary lavender oil to the relaxing energies of amethyst will increase the advantages of this bath; however, it's not strictly necessary.

You will require:

- One medium to large amethyst.
- White or purple candle.
- Lavender vital oil (optional).

Directions:

- Light the candle and run the bath.
- When the tub is midway full, include the lavender oil (if using).
- When you are bathing, ensure you are with your amethyst and take deep breaths gradually, and launching tension on the exhale. When the tub is filled, put the amethyst on the flooring of the tub near you and kick back and unwind.
- Wait in the bathing tub for about 15 minutes. Drain the bath when you are prepared.
- Remain in the tub as the water drains, so that any staying negative energy will be receded from your body and the amethyst.
- Gently extinguish the candle.
- Be sure to charge the amethyst and clean before using it in any other fantastic working.

Spell to Resolve Legal Issues.

If you discover yourself in legal difficulty, whether it's an overdue parking ticket or something more serious, staying calm is vital. Amethyst's ability to assist solve disputes and stop confrontational energies can help you find a resolution to your legal matters in a peaceful way. To prepare for this work, you may want to attempt the bath spell above.

(" Bath Spell for Patience and Flexibility") before you start.

You will require:

- One little amethyst crystal point.
- White candle.
- Two small muslin or other material squares.
- Needle.
- Blue thread.
- Orange thread.

Directions:

- Light the candle and take a couple of moments to quiet your mind.
- Insert the amethyst on top of one of the small material squares and put the other square on top of it.
- Beginning with the orange thread, sew the material squares together to confine the amethyst. As you sew,

display as factually as you can on the scenarios surrounding your legal concern.

- Use blue thread on your needle and stitch around the edges of the material again, this time concentrating your energy on clear communication, reality, and the peaceful resolution of your conflict.

- Put the appeal in front of a burning candle and state the following words:

" The powers of reality and reconciliation now infuse this wonderful development.".

- Permit the candle to stress out by itself.
- Place the amethyst in your pocket or bag when satisfying with an officer, attorney, or judge to help you focus your intent and bring about truthful and positive interaction.

Anti-Theft Travel Protection Spell

When checking out unknown places, specifically congested cities, it's always smart to keep a close eye on your belongings. You can likewise use a little bit of magic for some additional defense from those who would make the most of tourists.

This spell uses amethyst to protect you and your valuables from thieves so you can thoroughly enjoy your experiences. You can triple this spell or double as needed so that one charged amethyst is inside each of your luggage.

You will need:

- One amethyst per piece of travel luggage.
- Black spell candle.

Guidelines:

- Turn the candle on
- Place the amethyst on your hands and, merging your power to that of the Earth, conjure a sense of positive, protective energy.
- Focus this sensation unto the crystal.
- Watch the amethyst popping out a purple light serving as a protective glow from inside your suitcase (or knapsack).
- Expand the light so that it instills all of your items, then see it enveloping the entire travel box.
- When you believe the amethyst is wholly charged, then seal the energy by uttering the following words (or similar):.

"I pass through this world in peace and safety with all my personal belongings protect in my possession.

Let this be.".

- Keep the amethyst in front of the candle up until the candle has burned down.

- Then place it in your travel bag or sack throughout your journey.

- You can use that visualization to recharge the amethyst at any point throughout your journey if it feels required.

CHAPTER NINE

Citrine

This is another crystal typically found in magic and gemstone stores, this variety of quartz was called "citron" by the French just because of its similarity to a ripe lemon. Citrine is present in a variety of colors from pale yellow to dark amber, varying based on the amount of iron in the quartz crystal.

One traditional label for citrine is "the Sun Stone," due to its joyful color. Many citrine shine in the sunlight due to particles inside the stone, and the energy of this crystal is visibly positive, bringing the essence of sunshine in the form of joy, contentedness, and happiness. In reality, citrine has commonly been offered as presents to newborn babies for them to find a lifetime of emotional confidence and physical health.

Citrine was also called "the Merchant's Stone," understood to business people as a lucky talisman to be kept near the money register. A unique feature of citrine's wealth or commercial properties is that it not just assists you in obtaining wealth but also to maintain it. While other magical tools require the creation and build-up of riches, citrineenables the user to hang on to what they already have so it doesn't slip through their fingers.

Citrine'sconnection with the Planet Mercury as well as the element of Air, along with its yellow color, makes it an outstanding stone for magic having to do with concentration, visualization, decision-making as well as mental clarity in general. Communication issues and self-expression are also appropriate objectives when using this crystal. Anything needing a banishing of negativity and a boost in positive feelings can benefit from citrine, as this truly is a happy, uplifting stone.

In this chapter, you'll find out how to use citrine to energetically enhance the quality of your dreams, stay safe and secure in your finances, and rise above fear.

Cleansing Ritual with Citrine Stone

As with all of the standard magical tools, it's crucial to keep your crystals and other mineral stones clear of old, undesirable energies. There are lots of methods to clean your stones, but one basic approach is to use the purifying, fiery powers of citrine.

For excellent outcomes, clean raw and sleek stones independently, as jagged points or edges of natural stones might leave scratches in the polish. Make sure your citrine is charged and energetically clear before using it to clean your other stones.

The ritual is best done regularly, maybe once in a month on a bright day, or the eve of the Full Moon.

You will need:

- One medium to large piece citrine
- Large bowl
- Stones to be cleaned

Directions:

- Place the stones you would like to clean in the pan and place the citrine on top.

- Now, concentrating on your intention to clear unwanted energy, gently swirl the crystals together clockwise, using both hands.

- Repeat this twelve times to cleanse and get rid of unwanted energies present.

- After you have completed twelve swirls, remove the crystals from the bowl, and return the citrineright to your Altar.

- If you like, you may leave the cleansed stones out in the sun or moonlight for several hours to charge them with new natural energy.

Citrine Nightmare-Blasting Spell

For anyone who suffers from nightmares or undesirable dreams, citrine can work wonders. The brilliant energy of this crystal is like the Sun rupturing through the clouds, bring back color to the formerly grey landscape of your sleep. (In truth, you don't have to have "bad" dreams to gain from citrine-- try sleeping with a little piece under your pillow for a couple of nights and see if you don't see more pleasant, vivid adventures in your sleep!).

This spell uses citrine over the pineal eye, the spot above, and in between your seeing eyes that corresponds to your intuition. Integrating your intuition capabilities to clear stress from your body with the energies of citrine is an excellent way to enhance the quality of your dream experience.

This spell is most reliable when used before bedtime.

You will require:.

- One small piece of citrine.
- Fabric headband.

Directions:

- Put the citrine over your third eye and support it with the headband. Then lie on your back and take three deep breaths, focusing only on breathing in and breathing out.

Keep moving up through your body one part at a time-- calves, thighs, hips, bowels, stomach, chest, hands, lower arms, shoulders, neck, and face. Simply acknowledge any form of tension you feel in any of those parts of your body— do not make any judgments or worry about them. Just be a neutral observer of the energy existing in your body.

- Now envision an intense, pleasant yellow light moving and getting in from the soles of your feet. See it taking a trip up throughout your body, wiping out any stress you found during the very first part of the cleaning procedure. Take the necessary time you need to make this visualization reliable, and repeat it as many times as you wish.
- When you feel relaxed, you can get rid of the citrine from your third eye and place it under your pillow.

- Have a deep sleep, and enjoy much better dreams than you have had in ages!

Citrine Spell for Maintaining Wealth

The ancient people of every culture saw the Sun as the source of abundance and prosperity, which might be relied on at the beginning of each new day. Citrine's association with the Sun makes it an excellent agent of security and long-term abundance.

When you work this easy spell, you declare your appreciation for what you already have, in addition to your receptivity to more wealth to come.

You will require:.

- One little piece of citrine.
- One dollar bill.
- Green or black ribbon or thick thread.
- Small drawstring bag.
- Work candles for the environment (optional).

Directions:

- Light the candle.

- Hold the citrineappropriately in your dominant hand and the dollar bill in your second hand.

- Take a deep breath as you focus your energy on merging the power of the citrine with the dollar bill and the yellow light, which signifies your current level of wealth.

- Then, wrap the dollar bill firmly around the citrine.

- Next step is to secure the dollar bill with the ribbon or thread, while chanting the following (or comparable) words until you have put it tightly in the right place:

" I hereby open the path to great wealth without any end."

- Put the wrapped citrine in the drawstring bag and keep it near your safe, checkbook, fireplace, or somewhere else in your house that symbolizes wealth.

Spell for Transmuting Fear

Many people have to wrestle with fear at one time or another-- even Witches with the power of magic at their disposal. Whether you're facing a terrible monetary or health catastrophe, having to conquer a fear like the fear of flying, or fear for somebody else you care about, there's a limitation to the usefulness of fear.

Fear is only significant for prompting us to run out of burning buildings or preventing strolling alone during the night in harmful locations. To put it mildly, fear helps support sound judgment. Beyond that, and specifically in situations we can't manage, anxiety just disrupts clear thinking and informed decision making. This spell is used to transmute the energy of fear from your energy field by grounding it into the Earth, restoring you to calmness, and the capability to trust in the Universe.

Obviously, not all worry has an apparent source, and it's not uncommon for individuals to be living their lives while stunted by a more generalized fearful sensation. This is especially real for those who are bombarded by adverts, news stories, and other media that broadcast afraid messages daily.

Attempt adding a freewriting session to this spell if you discover that you are being fearful but can't recognize the cause. You can seek help from the Universe in finding whether there's something buried in your subconscious, whether you're merely getting the fearful energies of the dominant culture at large without understanding it.

This spell is preferably applied with raw citrine, rather than polished so that there's absolutely nothing in between the surface area of the stone and the Earth when you bury it. If you only have polished citrine, do not let that stop you!

You will require:

- One piece of citrine.
- White candle.
- Spade or little shovel.
- Journal or composing paper (optional).

Directions:

- Light the candle.
- If you include the composing component, invest 10 to 15 minutes composing about the fearful sensations you're planning to transmute.
- When you've reached a satisfying response to the question "what am I afraid of?", then you're all set to proceed to the next important step.
- Having the citrine between your palms, close your eyes, and take three deep breaths.
- Now, speak your fears into the stone. You can state them as loudly or as silently as you wish-- whatever makes you feel comfortable, however, you do require to speak (or whisper) out loud.
- Gently extinguish the candle as soon as you have released your fears into the citrine.

- Use the shovel or spade to bury the citrine outside, allowing the Earth to absorb your fear energy and transmute it to neutral voltage.

- Thank the Earth for getting involved with you in this work.

- For best results, do this action instantly after extinguishing the candle.

CHAPTER TEN

Moonstone

Moonstone is most likely one of the most captivating beautiful stones in any Wiccan's collection. The most significant deposits of moonstone are found mainly in Sri Lanka and India but found in other parts of the world

Moonstone was highly regarded in ancient Rome, where individuals wore the stone in numerous forms of precious jewelry. The ancient Egyptians likewise revered the moonstone, relating it with the goddess known as 'Isis.'

As a significant member of the feldspar family, moonstone is abundant, but the gorgeous specimens are ending up being a growing number of uncommon due to high demand. Moonstone ended up being extremely popular throughout the Art Nouveau duration, where it was included in a plethora of fashion jewelry pieces, and men even used moonstone in their cufflinks and view chains.

In recent times, the mineral has seen a resurgence of appeal in the fashion jewelry world, which may put the most sparkling pieces out of reach for a number of the amazingly inclined. However, you don't need to have the most lovely moonstone to work with its powerful magical energies!

The Moonstone's planetary association, with Water as its essential Element. So, this makes it a great stone to work within any spell related to tranquility, or feminine intuition, as well as any ritual honoring the Goddess. Fertility magic is a natural opportunity for using moonstone, as is any working related to women's reproductive health, renewing romantic enthusiasm, and increasing psychic receptivity.

Traditionally, moonstone was also used for security and safety while traveling at sea. In this regard, you'll find a spell below that is useful for having safe travel on or over water, in addition to periods to support efforts to develop a child, stimulate a long-term relationship, and motivate prophetic dreaming.

Water Travel Protection Spell

Travel by sea is not as frequent as it was centuries back when the custom of getting in touch with moonstone for safe passage over water would have been commonly practiced. Nonetheless, moonstone's watery energy is ideal for a modern-day variation of invoking travel defense, whether you're headed to the beach, going on a cruise, flying overseas, or going along a river.

Mugwort's association with the Moon makes it a perfect herb to accompany the moonstone for protection. If you are unable to find mugwort, you can replace it with another security herb, such as the bay leaf or valerian.

You will need:

- Three small moonstones
- One teaspoon fresh or dried mugwort
- Little drawstring bag
- Work candles for the environment (optional).

Instructions:

- Light the candle, if using.
- Hold the moonstones between your palms and envision the beams of the Moon getting in each stone. See the white rays of light coming in contact with the rocks and charging them with the use of protective energy that will develop a magical guard around you through your journey over water.
- Put the charged stones in the drawstring bag, and sprinkle the mugwort over them while saying the following (or comparable) words:

"As the Moon casts a glowing course across the sea, I will now surround me the energies of defense will.".

- Shut the drawstring bag and leave it under moonlight overnight, either outdoors or in a windowsill.
- Go along with it for extra safety on your travels.

Spell For Enhancing Fertility.

Deciding to bring a new soul into existence can be exciting and somewhat tricky for a couple. Sometimes, making a baby does not occur instantly, and each passing month might bring about a new level of frustration. The resulting stress and anxiety can negatively affect fertility.

Moonstone is a useful, excellent ally when you are ready to become a parent. This easy, however effective spell can relieve any fear about the ability to conceive and therefore boost fertility. As a bonus offer, moonstone is associated with the defense of women during pregnancy also.

You will require:

- One little piece moonstone.
- Needle and thread.
- Tee shirt or other often-worn product of clothing.
- Small square of green fabric.

Instructions:.

- Center yourself in the moment by positioning the moonstone in your hands and breathing deeply.
- Visualize your intent streaming into the stone.

- See yourself as a mother and father, inviting a new life into the world.

- Turn the shirt or other item of clothes inside out and place the moonstone in an area that won't get in your method when you wear it when you're prepared.

- Place the green square of material over it and stitch it onto the clothing. As you sew around the edges, consider the moonstone pouch as a womb for your intents to develop a kid.

- When you have entirely encased the stone in the garment, spend a minute holding it in your hands and state the following (or comparable) words:

"I invite you, a new kid of mine, into this life."

- Place on the clothes and use it for the staying part of the day. Leave the stone in your unique pouch and wear the clothing frequently.

- You can eliminate or take out the pouch and sew the fabric firmly when you've conceived over the stone to make it into a keepsake for your new child.

Moonstone Spell for Rekindling Passion.

Every relationship needs a boost of renewed passion at one point or another. Attempt working with captivated jewelry to breathe brand-new life into your present love regimen if you find yourself getting in a less-than-passionate stage with your partner. This working is best executed under a waxing or full moonlight.

You will require:.

- One moonstone locket.
- Red candle.

Directions:

- Light the candle.
- Hold the moonstone locket in your hands and take a moment to keep in mind times when you felt enthusiastic about your partner, and times when your partner demonstrated the same sensations towards you.
- Picture a new encounter with your partner that revives the energies. If you find just a single stone in the necklace, focus more on holding that single stone as you think about the past and future enthusiasm in your relationship.
- Repeat the process with each one if the pendant has more than one moonstone.
- When you have totally charged your locket with passionate energies, put it on, close your eyes, breathe deeply, and enable yourself to take pleasure in anticipation of manifesting your desires on the real airplane.
- Gently extinguish the candle.

- Use the locket on your next date or other quality time with your partner.

Moonstone Dreaming Spell.

When we're living hectic, busy lives, our dreams can often look like merely a string of ridiculous "brain garbage" that don't cause much in the way of insight. However, typically, dreaming is suggested to be an automobile for essential messages from deep space and our more fabulous selves.

There are lots of crystals that can help clear out the mess of our subconscious and smooth out the course to help us have more profound, more lucid, and even prophetic dreams. Moonstone happens to be one of the most powerful stones for dreaming, as its energies are connected with the shifting, psychic tides of the Moon.

The spell calls for surrounding yourself with moonstone, producing an energy grid that will help you link to the heavenly plane in your sleep. You can take it an action even more if you like, asking for specific guidance to come to you in your dreams on the night you work the spell.

You will require:.

- Four small moonstones.
- Silver candle.

- Journal or composing paper.

Directions:

- Light the candle and spend a couple of minutes silencing your mind.
- If you have any particular challenge or problem that you would like to have resolved in the dream, write it on a sheet of paper (at the top).
- Hold the moonstones purposefully in your hands and visualize your personal energy instilling them up until they radiance. Quietly ask the stones to harness the power you require to receive dreams that include beneficial details.
- Now, keep one piece of moonstone on the floor at each corner of your bed. As you put each stone, state the following words (or something similar):

" By the light emerging from the Moon, my dreams will stream and tell me all I need to understand. So be it."

- Gently snuff out the candle before going to sleep.

- Keep the journal or composing paper (and pen) near your bed so that you can record your dreams very first thing after waking.

CHAPTER ELEVEN

Carnelian

Carnelian is a range of chalcedony quartz, colored with reds, oranges, ambers, and browns by impurities of iron oxide. Its dynamic colors look like that of a sunset, which made it the description "sunset confined in stone" in the old Egypt.

Take care if buying online; however, as some carnelian stones are agates, which have been heated and dyed.

Found mostly in India but also in South America and Madagascar, this stone has been used for countless years to safeguard against evil energies. It was made use of by the ancient Egyptians as a sign of the goddess Isis to secure against anger, jealousy, and malice, in addition to for renewal and vigor. Therapists throughout these times used carnelian to aid with blood problems. This stone was likewise part of ancient Eastern burial routines, frequently accompanying the dead as a protective talisman.

A stone fittingly connected with the Sun and the Element of Fire, carnelian can be used to boost one's nerve and express one's individuality without aggression. Speaker, stars, and entertainers of all kinds can benefit from its energy, as suggested by two standard labels for carnelian: "the Actor's Stone" and "the Singer's Stone."

Nevertheless, you need not be "natural" on phase to take advantage of the confidence- giving powers of this stone, anybody finding themselves having to provide a discussion or speech can contact the carnelian to help them succeed, no matter just how much they might fear the job.

Carnelian is one of the high protection spells, for as sunshine clears away shadows, this stone's energy eradicates negativity. Below, you will find spells for protecting versus negative energies, motivating positive self-expression, enhancing creative energy, and honing focus and concentration.

Empath's Spell for Banishing Harmful Energy
In the grand plan of things, being an empath is a blessing and a present. Still, it can likewise be a threat, as ultra-sensitive types can get slowed down, depressed, nervous, and even physically ill from too much exposure to lower vibrational, harmful energies. Whether it's due to staying in a hazardous workplace day, being the subject of another person's angry or hostile thoughts, or merely being in a physical space where past catastrophes have occurred, it's not unusual for Wiccans and other beautiful people to end up being adversely impacted by the type of energy around them.

The bold power of the carnelian makes it an outstanding stone of security against the negative impacts of all kinds. To increase the overall result of the spell, try taking a ritual cleaning bath and smearing yourself with sage, lavender, or other purifying herbs before you begin.

You will require:

- One piece of carnelian
- Small bell or chime
- Black candle

Directions:

- Light up the black candle and then sit in a comfortable chair with your feet flat on the ground.
- Holding the carnelian in between your palms, take a moment to concentrate on your physique and set a desire for clearing up your energy field.
- Put the carnelian properly on the floor close to your feet. Beginning with the soles of your feet, visualize any negativeness surrounding your feet and ankles being absorbed by the carnelian stone. (This energy might take the kind of dark, wispy, smoke like-tendrils in your mind's eye.).
- Next, position the carnelian in your lap. Imagine it cleaning your calves, thighs, and hip area in the same way.
- Bring the carnelian close to your chest to clear the upper torso and repeat the visualization.
- Place it near your throat to clean your shoulders and neck area.

- Finally, position the carnelian on the top of your head to cleanse your whole self and your surrounding aura.

- When you're completed, thank the stone and put it in front of the candle. Sounding the bell or chime over the sand to clear and recharge its energy, then gently extinguish the black candle.

- Place the stone in a location where you will stroll past it numerous times a day, so you can be reminded that you are protected from any unwanted energy.

Self-confidence Speaking Spell for Introverts.

Lots of people who are quite articulate in a one-on-one setting discover themselves unwilling to speak in group scenarios, whether it's a college class, a conference at work, or perhaps a social night out.

If this describes your personality, try bringing this simple appeal with you the next time you're communicating with others. You just might be shocked by the difference it makes!

You will require:

- One little piece of carnelian.
- Yellow, orange, or white candle.

Instructions:.

- Light the candle and spend a long time quieting your mind.

- Think of a recent period when you had something to contribute to a conversation, but kept it to yourself rather than sharing.

- Now pick up the carnelian and envision the scene once again; however, this time, see yourself stating what you desired to say. See the energy of your declaration spreading out light like a beacon throughout the environment of the scene.

- While still having a hold on the stone, repeat the following statement (or something similar)nine times:

"My voice has strong value, and other people will hear me."

- If you wish, think of another scene to "reword" in this way, and after that, repeat the statement nine more times. Then, continue this process until you feel a shift of confidence in your energy.

- Bring the carnelian with you next time you are in a group setting and watch as you begin to communicate your thoughts and ideas with confidence.

Spell to Spark Creativity.

Whether you're a writer handling author's block, an artist suffering from a lack of new ideas, or just wanting to shake things up a little in any innovative area of your life, this ritual is exceptional for reconnecting with your individual "muse." It's likewise excellent for merely unwinding and carrying yourself out of the everyday grind and into playful, magical co-creation with deep space.

The carnelian energy on your paper as you allow your right-brained consciousness to stream makes this crystal an actual "touchstone" linking you to the more magnificent worlds of creative manifestation.

Keep in mind: this spell has absolutely nothing whatsoever to do with artistic talent, so do not be intimidated if you're not the "artist" type. If you're someone who is always stating things like "I'm not artistic" or "I'm not truly imaginative," then you need to work this spell as often as possible!

You will require:

- One-piece carnelian Orange candle
- White paper.
- Markers, crayons, paints, or drawing pencils.
- Music (optional).

Guidelines:.

- Light up the candle and put on some music that motivates you in some method, if you wish.
- Place the paper and drawing/painting on the altar or table in front of you.
- Keep the carnelian stone anywhere on the paper.
- Just allow your drawing tool to swirl and move throughout the page freely, without thought or concern for producing a gorgeous piece of art. No one will see your development (unless you want them to).

- Carefully snuff out the candle when you feel that you are done.

- You can place your piece of launched creativity on your altar, ultimately view, fold it up and put it someplace discreet, and even get rid of it if you wish.

- Repeat this ritual whenever you need to spark a creative burst of energy for a task, or simply wish to participate in magical have fun with the Universe.

Spell for Beginning a Long-Term Project.

Whether you're composing a term paper, assembling a presentation, or even preparing to move home, it can be simple to get lost in the details of a big, multifaceted job. This basic spell helps you stay grounded and focused as you move through the different phases of your career.

If you haven't currently, take the first few minutes of the spell to make a list of the specific jobs that comprise your general task, taking this step will help you decrease any feelings of overwhelm, even before you finish the spell.

You will need:.

- One-piece carnelian.
- Orange ribbon or thick thread.
- One piece of writing paper (optional).
- Many post-it notes or small squares of paper.
- Work candle for atmosphere (optional).

Directions:

- Light the candle, if using. Invest some time quieting your mind, and after that create the "to do" list discussed above, either on paper or mentally.

- Now, jot down one task per post-it note, developing a stack of specific, workable jobs that will amount to the completed job.

- Put them in the order of what to be done first, second, third, and so on (without getting too hung up on private information, as you wish to be able to be versatile)

- Place the carnelian in between your palms, close your eyes, and spend a couple of moments envisioning the completed job. How will you feel when you're finished?

- When you have developed a stable, confident feeling about finishing the task, open your eyes, and state the words below (or something similar):.

"Step by step, one after the other, these tasks of mine will soon be done. So be it.".

- Place the carnelian right on top of the stack of notes, and put the pile on your desk or some other location where you will see it frequently while you work.

- As you total each task, take the corresponding note from the stack under the carnelian and tear it up into pieces.
- Take pleasure in enjoying the stack grow smaller sized and take convenience in the energies of the carnelian, assisting you in pushing on to the next action.

CHAPTER TWELVE

Bloodstone

Its common name would appear to suggest a mainly red coloring; bloodstone is, in fact, a deep green form of jasper with flecks of red and brown caused by iron oxide pollutants in the stone. The name "bloodstone" comes from Christian folklore, which holds that the blood from the crucifixion of Jesus spattered onto the green jasper stones below the cross. This mineral was also called "heliotrope" to the ancient Greeks, which translates approximately to "sunstone."

For many years, bloodstone has been used by various cultures to recover and ground the body through its purification and detoxification homes. The ancient Mésopotamiensusually dipped the stones in cold water and applied them to the skin over essential organs for detoxification. Also, Bloodstone was ground to a powder form and mixed with honey to draw out snake venom after a bite.

As a well-rounded promoter of vibrant physical health, bloodstone was believed to have the ability to reduce or stop bleeding arising from injuries. Perhaps this is the reason why warriors wore the stone for an additional increase of courage and protection throughout the battle.

Aligned with the planet Mars and the component of Fire, bloodstone supports spells focused around resolving negativeness and can be used to bring positive energy into any scenario. Indeed, as a green stone, it can continuously be included in cash spells for an additional increase, and it has also been used in magic associated with weather.

The spells below use the residential or commercial properties of bloodstones to assist one to recognize and avoid deception, strengthen relationships between kids and mothers, gain defense from bullies, and make difficult choices.

Bloodstone Deception Detection Spell

This spell works in scenarios where you're unsure you can trust what you're being told, whether it's at work, a social gathering, or perhaps within a relationship. Bloodstone resolves negativity and opens up access to personal assistance, while the color blue is related to genuineness, truth, and fidelity. As you carry this bloodstone beauty with you, it will continue to assist you in seeing the fact more clearly and accurately.

You will need:

- Blue spell candle
- Blue thread
- One small piece bloodstone
- Small square of a blue fabric

Instructions:

- Light up the candle.
- Place bloodstone right on top of the blue material on your altar or table.

- Place both of your hands right above the stone and focus on surrounding the stone with the dark blue light of fact.
- When it seems you have filled the stone with your energetic light, repeat the following (or similar) words three times:

"I distinguish between reality and untruth. I am secured from deceptiveness."

- Wrap the bloodstone thoroughly in the material, secure it with the blue thread, and place it in front of the candle.
- Allow the candle to stress out by itself.
- Take the charmed stone with you in your pocket or purse to help secure yourself from all forms of deception.
- You may also hold it in your hand or while in your pocket during discussions to feel whether or not you are being tricked.

- Charge it with the above routine whenever you feel the requirement.

Spell to Strengthen The Mother and Child Relationships

The bond existing between a mother and her child is profound and spiritual; however that does not imply that conflict between the two will not take place periodically (or frequently!), particularly at certain phases in life. This spell assists in strengthening the loving energy between mother and kid, and the gift can be given as a method of calming an existing dispute or avoiding a future one.

Bloodstone is related to motherhood, which makes it an exceptional focal point for this beautiful working; however, you can replace another crystal if you wish.

Considering that this is a present rather than a beauty you use yourself, it's essential to be mindful of your intentions here. This working is not about controlling the ideas or behaviors of another person, but about fostering caring energy between 2 individuals. The difference is essential, so if you're in genuinely hostile conflict with your mom and are not able to summon calm, caring sensations, then this is not an excellent spell for you to operate at this time.

You will need:

- Bloodstone precious jewelry (such as a ring, bracelet, pendant, and so on)
- Pink candle

Directions:

- Place the bloodstone fashion jewelry on the table or altar in front of you and light the candle.
- Hold the precious jewelry carefully between your palms.
- Then, visualize yourself with your mother (or anyone else to whom you want to strengthen a bond with). See yourself communicating in a calm and tranquil way.
- Visualize yourself taking a deep breath when you feel your feelings increasing, or politely excusing yourself to be able to take a minute to soothe yourself before returning to the conversation.
- After the visualization, infuse the necklace with relaxing energy as you state the following (or similar) words:

"As above, so below

Our relationship continues to grow.

As below, so above

Our communication is filled with love

So be it."

- Provide the charmed jewelry as a present for a birthday or holiday or as an "even if" present.

Anti-Bullying Protection Spell

When facing their challenger, warriors of the past were known to wear a bloodstone amulet close to their hearts to provide the courage. The red specks of intense Mars energy integrated with the deep Earthy green hues imbue a feeling of well-fortified security. This protective amulet can protect you from if you're in the regrettable scenario of dealing with somebody who acts in a bullying way towards you their negativeness. You'll quickly be well out of their radar and left alone because bullies only target individuals they believe they can have a result on. This protective magic at its finest!

If you do not have a pendant including bloodstone, you can make one by wrapping the wire around the stone and connecting it to any kind of pendant cord You can also find simple cables with small wire "baskets" that permit you to put crystals of your choice inside them, successfully serving as an all-purpose crystal pendant.

You will need:

- One bloodstone locket or pendant
- Black spell candle

Instructions:

- Light the candle.
- In a sitting position, place the locket or pendant in your lap.

- Begin by envisioning a beautiful green orb sitting in the middle of your lap. See the sphere grow gradually as it envelops you within it. This is your unusual force- field, protecting you versus your opponent.

- On the external edge of this shielding energy, picture dynamic spots of red flaring up to caution away anyone who would do your damage.

- When you've summoned a peaceful, protected sensation, hold the bloodstone within your palms and say the following words (or something similar):

"I am secured from all who mean me damage, with the Heart of Earth and the Fire of Mars,

This amulet guards me against their gaze and sends them on their method. Let it be."

- Place the amulet right in front of the candle and permit the candle to burn out on its own.

- Use it around your neck whenever you might come into contact with those who would bully you.

Bloodstone Divination for Big Decisions

When you're facing a primary choice in life with lots of possible options, it can be challenging to get a clear answer from your instinct alone. During this spell, you will evaluate all of the possible outcomes of a decision and enable this beautiful stone to assist you in choosing which course to sail.

You will require:

- One small to medium piece of bloodstone.
- One blank and unlined sheet of paper.
- Pen or Black marker

Directions:

- Take some deep breaths and reflect quietly on the choice you have before you.
- Place the bloodstone in the middle of the paper.
- With the pen or marker, draw the line radiating outside from the stone for every one of your possible options. The edges should be separated at least an inch apart.
- Now take out the stone and hold it correctly in your hand.
- Next, close your eyes, take a long, deep breath, and then roll or drop the stone in the middle of the paper, bearing in mind where it lands.
- The line's closest to (or straight on) the option you're being asked to think about.
- Inspect with your gut; you will get a definite yes or no on this specific option. Repeat the procedure as required until the final choice is clear

CHAPTER THIRTEEN

Jade

The stone we refer to as jade involves two different minerals that have extremely comparable residential or commercial properties. Jade has been used in many cultures for making a variety of items varying from ax heads to incense burners to fashion jewelry.

Jade is among the most revered stones of magic; numerous traditions have honored its powers from a long time to the present moment. Holding the stone firmly in the palm of their ideal hands, ancient traders would count on its capabilities to make the most effective possible choice throughout business transactions. In China, jade has long been thought to harness and hold the power of all five of the Chinese virtues of humanity: benevolence, knowledge, righteousness, propriety, and fidelity. You can observe symbols of all five of the attributes sculpted into jade stones throughout China.

The Mayans and Aztecs also carved pictures of their deities out of Jade and used it for its medicinal qualities. Known across the world as a stone aligned with the bladder and kidney, Jade has been called by many unique names, such as the spleen stone, yu stone, stone of the loin, piedra de hijada, as well as the stone of flank. In recent times, people take Jade to support the immune system throughout times of tension.

Jade is also aligned with Element of Water, the planet Neptune and its restorative energy supply relaxing vibrations that cover the user in a shield of protective energy. Jade promotes knowledge, balance, and peace and is particularly helpful during difficult times in life. This stone can help clear out old psychological patterns to bring clearness to a complicated scenario. Some of the magical uses for Jade include security, new love, abundance, gardening, and dream work. The spells below use Jade to promote balance and prosperity, assist with fast decision making, and deal with the feelings of guilt.

A Spell to Restore Balance

Typically, when we hear the word "stress," it raises unfavorable connotations. This is mostly as a result of the imbalances of mainstream modern life, where busyness rule the day, and the value of associating with the Earth and the spiritual realm is forgotten. Though, stress does have beneficial qualities in moderate quantities, as it helps us recognize when we are overworked, out of balance, or perhaps in some form of danger.

The Chinese symbol known as yin and yang represents the interconnectedness of all things and the balancing of opposites. This visual symbol of darkness within light and lightness within dark reveals to us that our Universe is made up of seemingly opposite yet complementary qualities, such as stress and ease, forcefulness, and patience, as well as gentleness and firmness.

This spell will help you bring back the balance within you, and works for times when you feel excessively stressed, irritable, or anxious.

You will need:

- Two pieces of jade.
- Yin-yang symbol (drawn or printed).

Directions:

- Place the yin-yang sign on the altar or table in front of you. Put one piece of Jade on either side of the image.

- Invest some time silencing your mind as you keep a mild focus on the symbol.

- Using your left hand, pick up the jade to the right of the symbol and hold it tight. Using your right hand, move up the Jade to the left and hold it so fast.

- Hold one closed palm across the white circle within the black half of the yin- yang, and the other across the black ring in the half of the white.

- Have three deep breaths in this place, and envision the power of the yin- yang paired with the energies of the jade stabilizing any anxiousness in your life. Consider any elements of your life that need more balance and ask the Universe to assist you in restoring equilibrium to those areas.

- Place the stones straight on the yin-yang sign when you are through with your contemplation.
- It's either you leave them on your altar or in another prominent place until you ascertain your balance has been brought back.

Spell for Prosperous Beginnings

Whether you're beginning a business, moving into a new house, starting a new task, or inviting a new member into your household, milestones like these are exceptional events for a little magic.

The scarab beetle was thought to be a sign of prosperity and rejuvenation in ancient cultures ranging from Egypt to China. As a magical sign, it's an appropriate counterpart to Jade, which is highly valued as a success stone in the conventional Chinese system of Feng Shui.

You will need:

- Three small to medium pieces of Jade.
- Green spell candle.
- Potted plant.
- Image of a scarab.

Directions:

- Put the scarab image on the table or altar before you.
- Assemble the jade stones in a triangle around the scarab, and put the candle near the top rock.
- Light the candle and profess the words below (or similar):

" My success, luck, fortune accompany me on this new important journey.".

- Allow the candle to stress out itself.

- Bury the Jade around the potted plant and embellish the pot with the picture of the scarab.

- Place the plant in a prominent place where you will be constantly reminded of its thriving energy and the fantastic potential of the new beginning you are commemorating.

Spell for Resolving Feelings of Guilt.

Everyone feels guilt over a particular situation at some point in their lives. In some cases, this is because of the choices we've made that caused harm to another, but we might also have feelings of guilt even though we're not at fault. Whether it arises from misplaced blame or real wrongdoing, regret is a negative emotion that can sap us of happiness, essential wellness, and excellent health.

This spell will help you find the nerve to make apologies and reparations if suitable, or just enable you to move on and release the regret or guilt in your life. Because you will be put in the ground the jade, simple pieces are perfect, but you may still use refined jade if need be.

You will need:

- One or more pieces of raw jade
- Spade.
- Light blue spell candle
- Journal or writing paper (which is optional).

Directions:

- Light the candle and spend a few minutes contemplating the source(s) of your guilty feelings or feelings of regret. You may wish to write about it to get a clearer understanding of your role in a particular situation.
- Choose a jade stone and put it on your dominant palm when you're ready.
- Envision the situation, which has caused you to feel guilt.
- Close your eyes, and permit the jade to soak up this memory.
- Now, picture yourself making an apology, if required, and making any necessary reparations to correct the situation. Take the recovery energy of this pictured scenario and see it as a white light pouring into the palm of your non-dominant hand.
- Position your non-dominant hand over the jade. Depending on the intricacy of the situation you are working to heal, you may desire to repeat this procedure with additional jade stones.

- When you complete the ritual, bury the stone(s) in the Earth to let go of the formal feelings of guiltiness.

- If you need to apologize and amends to others, do so promptly to heal from the experience fully.

Split-Second Decision Spell

As a supporter of wisdom and clarity in fast-moving circumstances, jade is ideal for scenarios needing quick choices under pressure, whether on the task or in other areas of your life. One charged stone in your pocket or handbag can help you make every call with self-confidence.

You will need:.

- One medium piece jade.

Instructions:

- Grip the jade between your palms and take a deep breaths.

- Close your eyes and see yourself covered in quiet, peaceful energy. In this state, you can quickly access your personal assistance.

- Call a feeling of self-confidence and self-trust as you envision yourself making fast, accurate decisions that will have lasting positive results on the people.

- When you are ready, send this energy of calm self-esteem into the stone, and then state the following (or comparable) words:

  " As rapidly as I touch this stone, all I need for my choice is understood. So let it be.".

- Bring the jade with you in situations where you encounter the need to make decisions rapidly.

CHAPTER FOURTEEN

Malachite

It's groups of much lighter stones, and deep emerald greens creating a striking look, and its relative softness makes it a famous stone for sculpting into distinct shapes. This copper carbonite mineral was called by the ancient Greeks after the leaves of the mallow plant (or "Malachi" in Greek).

Malachite was mined in the Sinai area of Egypt since 4000 BCE. Related with wealth and travel, this was a well-known stone with ancient traders and merchants. Traders would use the stone while conducting a group in order to enhance the success of their deals. Merchants would keep malachite with their cash to increase their financial holdings. In many regions, malachite became called "the salesperson's stone." It was as well known for its protective nature, nevertheless, and was worn in some areas of Italy to ward off the wicked eye.

Among different ways, malachite has been used throughout the ages is purification. The intense green of the malachite stone absorbs negativeness and toxins from the body and the environment around us. The toxic substances of the earth, such as radiation, and the contaminants of the body, such as stomach pains, can both be extracted using the heavenly powers of malachite. Ironically, however, malachite is poisonous to the human body and must never be taken in an elixir or consumed in any form. To be on the safe side, deal with sleek malachite rather than its raw form.

Related to the world of Venus and the Element of Earth, the protective residential or commercial properties of malachite are quite strong. When there is an impending threat or splinter to alert of negative energies, the stone has been known to break. Malachite likewise helps to ward off headaches and diseases and is an especially excellent security stone for kids.

As a stone of improvement, it is used magically to help change psychological, physical, or spiritual circumstances from negative to favorable by removing the adverse energies. Wearing malachite on the skin helps attract love and make the user more ready to let love into their life.

Malachite is used in beautiful workings related to love, money, travel, defense, and boosting psychic abilities. It is stated that the stone will improve the incredible power of spellwork or prophecy. The spells listed below make use of malachite to safeguard sleeping children, lower road rage, calm fears of flying,

fend off unwanted electronic communications.

Roadway Rage Reduction Spell

For those who handle congested commutes to and from work, traffic can damage a favorable attitude. The people that know the Law of Attraction understand that getting frustrated tends to lead to even more discouraging circumstances!

This enjoyable little spell makes use of malachite's ability to reduce the effects of unfavorable circumstances to assist you in remaining calm, relaxed, and collected in any traffic scenario, leaving your ability to attract real situations undamaged.

You will require:

- One small malachite stone
- Small toy cars and truck
- White or yellow spell candle

Instructions:

- Place the malachite and the small toy automobile in the middle of your altar or workspace.

- Get the stone and hold it in your dominant hand.

- Close your eyes and imagine yourself in your automobile on the open road. Permit yourself to feel the ease, pleasure, and liberty of taking a trip quickly and smoothly to your location.

- Take a couple of deep breaths as you allow this favorable vibrational frequency to take hold in your consciousness. Visualize the energy of this sensation, instilling the malachite with you.

- When you notice the stone is fully charged, put the stone on top of the toy car.

- Now, picture yourself stuck in traffic. As you discover the feelings of stress and anxiety and frustration start to appear, select up the malachite and allow the energy, you just charged it with to diffuse the negativity you've simply conjured. Keep in mind the difference in how you feel after holding the stone for sometimes.

- Return the stone on top of the car and light the candle as you say the following (or comparable) words:

" As the speed of traffic stops and begins

I remain centered in my heart.

No matter how the traffic's streaming

I always

ys get to where I'm going."

- Allow the candle to stress out itself.

- Keep the toy car in your glove section, and hold the malachite handy to keep whenever you wind up in heavy traffic.

Magical Malachite Message Minimizer

Since the advent of the "cell phone," the quantity of time we invest in dealing with texts, e-mails, and phone calls has more than quadrupled. (For those who likewise use social media, this interruption aspect is multiplied significantly!) All of this communication can result in a messy mind, making it harder to shift into a magical frame of mind at the end of the day.

The simplest solution is to leave the phone turned off, or silence informs for new messages when we desire a break, this isn't always possible. However, it is possible to reduce the "sound" related to undesirable, unnecessary contact with the cyber-world.

Contemporary techno-pagans have discovered that malachite works in safeguarding versus any unfavorable energies connected with our modern forms of communication. Use this spell to assist you in defending against the minor (or major) disruptions that undesirable e-mails, texts, and calls can trigger in the circulation of your everyday life.

Note that your intention ought to be focused on eliminating undesirable communication so that only people you want to communicate with will contact you.

You will need:

- One medium to sizeable malachite stone
- Phone (or computer system).

Guidelines:

- Put the malachite on your phone or computer.

- With your hand still touching the stone, imagine a shield of green light surrounding you and your gadget, avoiding any unwanted communications.

- See the grave green stone absorbing all unwanted, congested energy from your everyday interactions on this gadget and transmuting it into tranquil, quiet power.

- If you like, state the following (or comparable) words as you charge the stone with your power:

"Do not call, do not push 'send.' Unwanted messages now will end.

Let it be.".

- Leave the malachite on or near your gadget to continue to ward off unwanted interactions throughout the day.

Energy Protection Charm for Children.

Kids are little psychic sponges and are continuously detecting the moods and emotions of grownups, whether we understand it or not. Some kids are even more sensitive than others (particularly those who end up thinking about the magical arts!); however, all children are energetically susceptible to their surroundings to some degree.

Even the most loving moms and dads go through psychological struggles that can permeate into the subconsciousness of their children. This is all part of human advancement, but we can use magic to minimize the impacts our unfavorable energies have on the youths around us.

Malachite is traditionally referred to as a defense stone for kids. Making a malachite beauty to await your kid's room creates an invisible shield to keep out unwanted energies, entities, and anything else on the heavenly airplane that may cause unnecessary problems. It's perfect for hanging this beauty in a window so that it can charge daily in the sunlight. If this isn't possible, just make sure to charge the stone routinely, preferably in direct sunlight.

You will need:

- One small to medium piece malachite.
- 4 to 5 inches of thin wire.
- 8 to 12 inches of thick thread.
- Hook.
- Work candles for the environment (optional).

Guidelines:

- Light the candle, if in use.

- Spend some time calming your mind and breathing deeply. This is a particularly essential first step, provided the focus of this working, you don't desire any tension, worry, or other negative energy to be in your field as you charge this beauty and creativity.

- Hold one edge of the wire against the malachite and start covering the length around the stone.

- As you work, imagine the stone radiating favorable energy in the child's room and continuing over the window. See the power of the rock breaking through and dissipating any destructive power that could enter your child's unconscious mind.

- As an additional energetic increase, attempt singing or humming a lullaby while you protect the stone within the wire.

- Use the thread to make a wall mount for the stone with a loop.

- Put the hook on the window and hang the pendant in the sunlight (if possible), being mindful to hang it high adequate to be out of the reach of kids.

Spell to Soothe Fears of Flying.

Even in this modern-day age of frequent flight, the worry of flying is not unusual if this fear has kept you on the ground in the past, attempt using the protective, soothing energies of malachite to assist you to overcome your fear.

This spell includes getting in touch with the protective powers of a chosen divine being or other magical beings. If you deal with the God and Goddess, you can call on them directly for this spell, or discover an element of them amongst the ancient deities connected with journeys, such as Hermes, Apollo or Rhiannon. Additionally, you could request for the support of Archangel Raphael, who guards travelers. Call on the sylphs to keep you boosted and feeling safe during your flight if you work with the Elementals.

You will need:.

- Two small to medium malachite stones.
- Sheet of white paper.

Directions:

- Take three deep breaths and imagine a white light burning from your stones
- Allow the light to grow on each inhale up until you are covered in a soft white glow.

- Turn the white paper to make a paper airplane when you're prepared to begin. You can fold your airplane in any design that you like.
- Put one malachite stone on each of the wings. Focus your energy and intent on the aircraft as you let it represent your upcoming travel.
- Now imagine yourself being brought on the wings of your selected excellent assistant(s). Imagine them carrying you gently through the sky, knowing that you are safe and can relax on their sides.
- Spend a few minutes holding quickly to this vision, and then place the stones on your altar up until your next journey through the air. You can keep the paper plane on the platform or recycle it as well.
- Bring the enchanted malachite with you in your pocket or purse for your next flight.

During launch (and during the flight, if need be), hold the stones to recall the safe and peaceful feeling you had during your visualization. Silently ask your picked excellent assistant(s) to stick near to you throughout the flight.

CHAPTER FIFTEEN

Tiger's Eye

Tiger's Eye is known as a macrocrystalline quartz, consisted of numerous interwoven layers of earthy browns and glimmering gold hues. The resemblance of the stones to a tiger's fur, in addition to the appearance of "eyes" in most of the smooth stones, resulted in the name of this mineral. As symbols of animals, tigers represent power, strength, and sophistication, and these attributes are associated with the stone also.

The ancient Egyptians used the tiger's eye stones as real eyes in sculptures of their goddesses and gods, representing the ability of the divine to see all and know all. In the East, the tiger's eye has long been connected with wealth and good fortune. Ancient Roman soldiers wore and carried the stones in battle, as they believed it had the power to make weapons bounce off of their armor. More substantially, these amulets provided the user nerve to stand up to an enemy on the fight field and defend what he thought was right.

Tiger's eye is useful for focusing the mind, bringing about clarity, improving spiritual visions, and supporting the required transformation that should happen throughout the journey of life. Associated with the Sun and the Elements of Earth and Fire, this stone is likewise used in functions for defense from psychic attack, wealth and prosperity, and great fortune in new endeavors.

Some individuals use the tiger's eye's animal connection to work magic for the security and preservation of tigers and other huge cats, both in the wild and in refuge parks. In this chapter, you'll discover spells using the tiger's eye to bring success to a new business endeavor, look for clearness in a murky scenario, and provide yourself with a boost of guts and bravery, along with a creative divination ritual.

Spell for a Successful New Business

Beginning a new business is a massive leap of faith, even for the most skilled entrepreneurs. This spell assists you in getting off on the best foot, adding an object of personal importance to you with three main features or qualities of the tiger's eye: wealth, excellent fortune, and success. You'll be putting in place a talisman to aesthetically advise you of your future success throughout every day.

You will need:

- Some small tiger's eye stones
- Journal or composing paper
- Green or gold candle
- Small dish, bowl, or cup that has personal importance

Directions

- Light the candle and take a few deep breaths.

- Invest a long time considering what "success" in your business appears like. Perhaps it's a shop full of customers searching the merchandise, or a significant personnel of well-compensated employees. You might visualize numerous five-star evaluations on a social network site, or satisfied customers were referring your business to their friends.

- Do some conceptualizing along these lines and make a list of many manifestations of "success" as you can think of. Be as precise as you can with the provided details.

- Now hold some of the tiger's eye stones in your hand and make a loose fist. Close your eyes and picture one of the manifestations from your list, being as abundant in detail as you can.

- Place the stone in the cup, bowl, or dish.

- Repeat this procedure with the remainder of the stones-- imagining your success and then putting the energy of it into the vessel.

- When you are done, find a particular area in your new company to put the vessel to ensure excellent fortune and success.

Refocusing Spell for Long-Term Projects

When dealing with long-term tasks such as academic papers or discussions, it's simple to get bogged down in the nitty-gritty information and lose focus, which makes it challenging to stay motivated. Even when taking a useful approach, such as beginning with the most favorable aspects and conserving the hardest parts for the future, there are overwhelming moments that can make finishing the work appear difficult.

In this spell, the tiger's eye represents the "all-seeing eye" that can view every angle of a situation. You will draw on its energies to rise above the information and see the project come together into a cohesive whole.

You will need:

- One medium to big tiger's eye stone
- One sheet of essential size yellow or blue paper
- Numerous small slips of paper

Directions:

- Place the tiger's eye in the center of the blue or yellow paper on your altar or work area.

- On every one of the sheets of paper, write a word or phrase that represents an angle of the task that you're battling with. These can be more significant concerns, such as meeting the task deadline, down to the smallest, most confounding information, such as how to rework a disorganized paragraph.

- As soon as you've written each issue on a sheet of paper, take a moment to focus your gaze on the tiger's eye. Imagine yourself taking a look at the task from a high vantage point and see it coming together as if being sewn with gold stitches by an unseen hand.

- Hold this vision for a few minutes and allow a sensation of self-confidence to develop within you.

- When you feel sufficiently definite about completing the job, collect all the sheets of paper and fold them into the yellow or blue paper.

- Place the tiger's eye on top of the folded paper and leave it on your table or altar up until you have completed the job.

Tiger's Eye Courage Spell

Tiger's eye empowered even the strongest Roman soldiers to be brave and bold during a fight. Just as the soldiers used the tiger's eye to deflect weapons wielded by the people attacking them, we can use the tiger's eye to deflect fear triggered by challenging social scenarios.

This spell will enable you to produce a metaphorical guard to bring with you into whatever battles you face, whether they involve having a hard conversation with your boss, dealing with daunting colleagues, or perhaps a vacation dinner with sone of your in-laws.

You will need:

- Four pieces of tiger's eye
- Little cloth bag
- Red spell candle

Directions:

- Take a couple of deep breaths and make yourself comfortable.

- Envision the approaching encounter you're concerned about. See yourself in the moment after the meeting has come to a close, feeling satisfied and relieved with the way you handled the circumstance. You don't have to visualize any of the details-- simply focus on the feeling of having successfully dealt with the challenge.

- When you're all set, light the candle. Place the very first stone in front of the candle and state the following words (or something similar):

" I honor myself for acknowledging my worries."

- Place the second stone behind the candle, straight in line with the very first, and say the following (or similar) words:
  " I trust my intuition to direct my words."

- Place the third stone to the right of the candle and say the following (or similar) words:
  " I verify my capability to interact with stability."

- Place the final stone to the left of the candle, directly in line with the 3rd, and say the following words (or similar):
  " I stand in my sovereignty no matter the actions of others."
  Allow the candle to melt.

- Gather the stones into the bag and keep it with you throughout the upcoming encounter.

- Visualize the stones creating a protective shield around you as you browse the conversation(s).

Scrying With The Use of Tiger's Eye
Tiger's eye has to do with both the Sun and the Earth, which makes perfect sense considering its interwoven layers of brown and gold. This stone is also a promoter of energetic interaction between the physical and spiritual realms.

This spiritual technique uses the shinning exterior of polished tiger's eye stones, in addition to water and sunlight, to assist in striking visual images that can communicate messages to the receptive practitioner. It is best carried out outside on a sunny day, but if this isn't possible, a warm or sunny window can also work.

You will need:

- Many (about 10 to 20) small to medium tiger's eye stones
- Writing paper or Journal
- Glass dish
- Sunshine
- Cup of water

Directions:

- Place the tiger's eye stones in the glass dish.

- Put the water over the stones until the dish is almost full (but don't let it spill over the edge).

- Have some deep breaths to clear your mind.

- Keeping your focus mild, gaze on the small pool of water and the reflections of the stones. Be open to any images or visions that develop.

- Try to record your images and ideas in your journal to explore further when you have finished.

CHAPTER SIXTEEN

Jet

Unlike the other crystals and stones included in this collection, the jet is a fossilized wood rather than a real gem. As the araucaria trees of the Jurassic duration began to die off, their rotting wood ended up in swamps, rivers, and other bodies of water. The wood was eventually flattened by the pressure of multiple layers of organisms and mud over millions of years. When grand tree into gleaming black stones, Chemical alters eventually morphed the residues of this.

Named from a region in Asia Minor, the color of this stone is the source of the phrase "jet black," used to describe anything as black as it is possible to be. Some specimens might, in fact, be browner in color.

Jet has been used because prehistoric times-- it has been found in burial mounds as far back as 1400 BCE-- and was treasured for its protective residential or commercial properties by ancient travelers and soldiers alike. It is a soft, dull stone in rare type; the jet can endure a high amount of polishing, which enables it to take on a mirror finish. It was frequently used for this function during medieval times.

It was also widely known in many cultures during this duration that breathing in the smoke from the burning jet was physically and spiritually useful. In more recent history, plane became well-known as a "mourning stone" after Queen Victoria of England used it while mourning the death of her other half, Prince Albert.

Like lots of black stones, jet gets rid of undesirable energetic attachments and soaks up negativeness. It's an excellent stone for meditation and recovery sorrow. Related to the planet Saturn and the Element of Earth, a jet is used in magical workings connected to filtration, psychic security and increased psychic awareness, promoting luck associated with money, and prophecy. Like malachite, it is known to increase the efficiency of magic when put on the altar or other work areas.

The spells listed below show you how to use the jet to develop a pendant to ward off headaches, to clean your aura, to support yourself during a time of sorrow, and to promote success at a brand-new job.

Anti-Nightmare Protection Charm

Jet is a terrific stone to use in sleep magic, specifically for those who experience nightmares or other sleep disturbances. Jet beads can be discovered through crystal and mineral retailers and at craft shops(though make sure to check at craft shops that you're not getting replica glass beads). If nothing else, you can buy a jet locket or bracelet and unstring it to create this sleeping beauty from scratch.

You will need:

- 10 to 15 jet beads
- A number of inches of thick silver thread
- Scissors
- Thumb-tack or hook
- Work candle for atmosphere (optional).

Guidelines:

- Light the candle.
- Spend a long time taking deep breaths and quieting your mind. Start by cutting a long piece of silver thread when you're ready.
- Connect a knot at the end of the thread, making it big enough that the jet bead will not slip off.
- Place one bead on the thread and state the following (or similar) words:

" Peaceful sleep I shall find, all my headaches, I now bind.".

- Connect a knot and then repeat the chant as you put the next bead on the thread. Repeat this process until all the beads have been strung.

- Use the scissors to cut the thread, leaving enough to tie a small loop. Use the loop to hang the pendant on a tack or hook above your bed.

Aura Purification Ritual.

Everyone has an aura, the subtle energy field that surrounds us and extends externally from our physical form. Our thoughts, actions, diet, and physical environment have an impact on our aura so that it changes depending on how we're thinking and feeling, and how we're treating our bodies and minds. Those who can see atmospheres can inform if an individual's overall energetic state is healthy or in requirement of assistance, based upon the vibrancy (or do not have thereof) of the colors swirling in their auric field.

You do not require to be able to see your aura, however, to know if you're energetical "down in the dumps." This spell uses the cleansing properties of a jet to clean dirty or stagnant energies in your auric field. Use it in conjunction with healthy food, workout, and regular meditation (or other spiritual activity) to keep your aura vibrant and lively.

You will need:

- Several (10 to 30) pieces of jet.

- Pillows.

- Small fabric bag (optional).

- Work candle for atmosphere (optional).

Guidelines:

- Light the candle, if using.

- Take three deep breaths and launch any little disruptions from your day on each exhalation.

- Lie down in a comfortable position on your flooring, using pillows to support yourself so that you can fully unwind.

- Place the jet stones around the boundary of your body, paying conscious attention to each positioning.

- Now take more deep breaths and start to cause your pineal eye, or" second sight.".

- Starting with your feet, psychologically scan each part of your body. As you move gradually up your body, be conscious of any part that feels stuck, dark, or otherwise less-than-optimal in terms of energy. Don't over examine this. Instead, let your intuition guide you.

- Imagine a white light over any location you feel is energetically deteriorated or out of balance, to send out power and energy back to that area.

- When you have finished a full scan of your body, feet, calves, knees, thighs, groin, intestines, stomach, chest, neck, arms, hands, and head, picture your entire body loaded with white light.

- Continue to lie there and relax completely for 10 to 15 minutes.

- You may wish to keep the jet stones in a small bag to use each time you need to clean your aura.

- Make sure to clean the stones in between uses, by smudging them with sage or smoke from a purification incense.

Routine for Easing Grief.

When someone you're close to hand down to the next world, it's essential to enable yourself to grieve. Grieving is a natural and healthy response to loss. But grief is a process, and eventually, it is necessary to let go of pain and progress with our lives. If you find that after much time has passed, you are not making development in this regard, a routine of memorial can help.

Jet's ability to assist with the purification of undesirable energies makes it an appropriate stone in this circumstance. Jet assists in increased psychic awareness, which can help you sense when your liked one is near, supplied you are open to it.

In this routine, you will be commemorating positive memories of your enjoyed ones. You will also be speaking of these memories aloud, as providing a voice to your experiences with this person will assist you launch sadness that has ceased to serve its purpose. If you are open to it, you might notice that your enjoyed one is listening, and adoringly appreciating your honoring of them in the physical world.

You will need:

- Several (10 to 20) jet beads.
- Pendant cord with clasp or thick thread.
- White candle.

Guidelines:

- Light the candle and take three deep breaths.
- Holding a jet bead in one hand and the locket cable or thread in the other, remember a pleasant memory of the person you are grieving. This can be a specific story, a character characteristic you admired in the person, or something joyful about your relationship with them.
- Speak out loud about this memory. If you feel likely, speak to the person.
- After speaking of the memory out loud, string the bead onto the cable or thread.
- Repeat this procedure for each of the jet beads.

- Protect the clasp or connect a knot in the thread when you have finished.

- You may wish to wear the beads as a pendant, place them on your altar, or hang them in a special place in your home.

- In the future, you might feel that it's time to let go of the string of beads or keep them in a place where you will not see them. This is fine, and ought to be taken as a sign that you have progressed substantially in your mourning procedure.

Jet Gifting Spell.

There are ethical concerns to be mindful of when it comes to working magic for others. Because everyone's course in life is genuinely their own, it's not up to us to cast spells for others without their approval, no matter how benevolent our objectives are. If you are asked to work a period for somebody else, then, by all means, do so. What if you want to provide a wonderful present to somebody who wouldn't think or understand in magic?

This spell is an excellent example of how you can share your beautiful talents with others without being unknowingly manipulative or needing their permission. It can be done with any stone for any function, however here we will deal with a particular custom offering jet to a person who has just landed a brand-new job.

Jet is a powerful beacon of best of luck, helpful energies, and personal calmness as well as stability under pressure. It is thought about the ideal gemstone to provide to somebody unique to honor their beginning in a new task. This necessary act is an excellent method to use your positivity and impressive skills to commemorate a pal and honor's or others enjoyed one's accomplishment. You can tell them that jet is a traditional best of luck stone for those who are beginning new tasks. Whether or not you inform them that you charged it with your own positive energy is up to you.

You will require:.

- Jet stone or piece of precious jewelry featuring jet.
- Small jewelry box.

Directions:.

- Place the jet stone or piece of fashion jewelry on the altar or table in front of you. Take a few minutes to concentrate on the recipient, noting the positive aspects of their character and the skills they will bring to their brand-new position. Picture them in their brand-new task achieving success and content.

- Concentrate your positive vibrations into the things by putting your hands above the jet.

- Place it in a little box when you have thoroughly imbued the stone with your positive and motivating energy.

- Offer the present to your friend or liked one and understand that each time they wear the precious jewelry or location the stone in a space at their new position, they will be filled with the good desires you have meant for them.

CHAPTER SEVENTEEN

Hematite

One of the common minerals on Earth is hematite, it was discovered in nations as far apart as Brazil, Norway, Italy, and Canada. In its pure type, hematite can typically develop into structures that appear to have petals like a flower.

The name hematite originates from the Greek word haimatites, which roughly equates to "blood," due to its ochre interior. In truth, for numerous centuries, hematite was called "bloodstone," though we now use that name for the green jasper featured previously in this book. A minimum of one misconception about the stone'sorigins was associated with the fight. As soldiers lay hurt in the consequences of a match, big pools of blood would collect and sink into the earth, forming the mineral.

Hematite's smooth, glasslike surface made it an ideal crystal for use as a primary mirror in ancient times. The powdered interior was used as a pigment in some cavern paintings, and by the ancient Egyptians who painted their pharaoh's tombs and sarcophaguses to illustrate pictures of the afterlife. Native Americans also used hematite to paint their faces before going into battle.

Despite its lots of associations with blood and battle, hematite is likewise understood as a stone linked to the higher mind. It helps to center and organize energy by grounding and relaxing the user. The ability to focus while experiencing numerous stimuli simultaneously can help to lower stress and anxiety in social situations. Associated with Mars and Saturn, and the Elements of Fire, Earth, and Water, hematite is used in beautiful functions related to grounding, psychic awareness, recovery, past-life recall, crucial and rational thinking, self- esteem and confidence, and dissipating unfavorable energy in one's environments.

The spells in this chapter use hematite to assist you in releasing concern endanger, transform pessimism into optimism, and ground yourself during social interactions that may trigger increased stress and anxiety.

Spell to Boost Optimism.

Anyone who comprehends the Law of Attraction understands that our ideas develop our reality. Hematite's grounding and healing homes can be used to help you turn your mindset around and go back to drawing in positive thoughts and experiences.

The hematite in this spell works on two levels. It helps you in reprogramming your unfavorable ideas into favorable declarations. It likewise wards off any other general unfavorable energy that you might have been unwittingly bringing in during your bout with cynical thinking.

You might be able to recognize a wide variety of unfavorable thoughts; it's best to just work with a small handful, to focus your objective on the act of transmuting the hostile into positive. Otherwise, you may get overwhelmed, or your focus might dissipate through the effort of rewriting a lot of separate ideas. Simply focus on the primary concerns that have been coming up for you repeatedly.

You will need:

- 3 to 5 hematite stones.
- 3 to 5 little slips of paper.
- White candle.

Directions:

- Light the candle and invest a long time quieting your mind.
- When you're all set to begin, recall a particular negative thought that you have been having recently.
- Among the slips of paper, rewrite the negative thought into a favorable statement. If you keep thinking, "I never

have any money," you can write, "I believe cash can stream to me without having to know its source.".

- Wrap the slip of paper around the hematite stone so that the words are dealing with the outside.

- Protect the paper with a drop of wax.

- Repeat this process with the remaining hematite and paper.

- Leave the paper-wrapped stones on your altar or place them in an area where you spend a lot of time, to assist you keep in mind to transform your negative thoughts into positive declarations.

- When you are downhearted, "funk" has raised, thank the stones and recycle the slips of paper.

Spell to Ease Social Anxiety.

Those who struggle with social stress and anxiety understand that it doesn't just occur in significant group circumstances. Depending on your level of sensitivity to other individuals' energy, anxiety can crop up throughout all sorts of encounters with other individuals.

In this spell, you will create a useful talisman to carry in your pocket, assisting you to keep in mind to ground and center yourself throughout social interactions.

You will require:

- One medium hematite stone.

- White or black spell candle.

Instructions:

- Light the candle and invest some time breathing deeply to peace your mind. When you feel ready, spend a few minutes imagining the sort of social situation that makes you uneasy.

- Ask yourself what activates an anxiety-producing reaction in your body during these scenarios.

- When you identify a trigger, get the hematite and hold it in between your palms.

- Take a deep breath in and out slowly, counting to 7.

- Imagine yourself in this imagined social setting, surrounded by white light. Repeat this breathing procedure three times, focusing on filling the stone with tranquil, relaxed energy.

- Now, place the hematite in front of the candle.

- Enable it to charge there till the candle has burned all the method down.

- Bring the charmed stone with you in your bag or pocket the next time you are participating in a social scenario that might produce a nervous reaction. You can hold on to the stone throughout any hard minutes without anyone even understanding!

Anger Release Spell.

Anger is a normal human feeling that fits, briefly, in specific scenarios. It's best for your health-- psychological, spiritual, and physical launch anger once it has served its purpose. This spell will assist you to remove the energy of sticking around bitterness and move on so that you can experience positive emotions, like hope, love, and joy, more completely and clearly.

Hematite's recovery homes and its ability to dissipate negativeness makes it an excellent stone for this sort of work. The Earth's power to transmute negative energy into positive or neutral energy is also made use of in this spell. Raw hematite is best for burying, but a sleek stone will likewise operate in a pinch.

You will need:

- Small to medium raw hematite stone.
- Black or white candle.

- Journal or writing paper (optional).

Instructions:.

- Light the candle, and invest some time quieting your mind.
- Allow yourself to focus on the anger and bitterness you're still carrying with you from an old scenario.
- If it assists, do some freewriting about the issue, try to determine the factors for the anger you're still feeling.
- Hold the hematite in between your palms when you're all set.
- Imagine the feelings you're wanting to release streaming into the stone, making it grow warm and more oppressive in your hands.
- Go outdoors and bury the stone in the Earth.
- As you dig the little hole and cover the stone, say the following (or similar)words:

" Let this bottled-up anger stop. These old sensations I now release. I blessed Be.".

Spell to Release the Habit of Worry.

Preparation ahead is a valuable skill to have in life, but continuously stressing about what might or may not occur is really detrimental to manifesting the truth you want. If you're a chronic worrier, you're certainly not alone.

However, you can empower yourself to ditch this practice with the help of the powers of Nature. The soothing effect of running water in this spell combines with the transmuting power of hematite to help you launch your routine of stressing and clear up your energy field for a smoother, more carefree life. You can put the stones in a bowl and run water from the sink or bathtub over them for many minutes and if you do not live near a stream or creek.

Spread the stones over the Earth. It's hugely recommended that you make an effort to bring them to a natural body of water, even if you have to go out of your method to get there.

You will require:

- Some raw hematite stones.
- Little cloth bag.

Instructions:.

- Spend some time quieting your mind.
- Take one stone and hold it between your palms when you feel prepared. Consider a specific concern that you are currently experiencing and let the hematite absorb the fears. Place it in the little bag.

- Continue this procedure with as many stones as you require. Bring the bag of hematite to a nearby stream, river, or creek.

- Sit silently for a couple of minutes at the edge and enable the sound and sight of the moving water to relieve your spirit.

- When you feel ready, carefully empty the bag of stones into the running water. Thank the Elemental spirits of the water for cleansing your energy of concern and fear.

- The next time you find yourself starting to anticipate something unfavorable happening in the future, return in your mind to the water running over the hematite stones.

- If you can, enter the practice of listening to recordings of a bubbling brook, a waterfall, or perhaps the ocean to assist you preserve a calmer mindset.

CONCLUSION

This marks the completion of the WiccaBook. You are now geared up with the necessary fundamentals and the knowledge to make your very first actions in the Craft and in understanding the fundamentals of the religion of Nature that is Wicca. The most excellent thing you can do for yourself is to acquire as much knowledge as possible on the Craft and Wiccan religion to train yourself in practice and to forge your journey with enjoyment and fulfillment.

Throughout your journey and through every step of the way, continuously remember the Wiccan Rede, "AN' IT HARM NONE, DO WHAT THOU WILT."